ONCE COWARD; FOREVER SPIRITUAL HERO!

ONCE COWARD; FOREVER SPIRITUAL HERO!

YHWH IS MY HEAVENLY FATHER, FOR I AM HIS SON, JESUS CHRIST!

MARKAIS RUBEN. C NEAL SR.

CONTENTS

DISCLAIMER

"These are my inner personal views as being Yahweh's chosen son, Jesus Christ!

My message is intended to bring all God's children together for the Spiritual realm, known as Heaven/eternal life.

The decision is now up to each individual believer, as my Heavenly Father, has given all humans free will." The choice is yours to decide!

Genesis 1:26:

Then God said, "Let Us make man in Our image, according to Our likeness; let them have dominion over the fish of the sea, over the birds of the air, and over the cattle, over all the earth and over every creeping thing that creeps on the earth."

1

HEAL WITH NEAL!

*The Jordan River, also known as the River Jordan, is located in the
Middle East and runs between the West Bank and the Kingdom of Jordan.*

Jordan River Baptism

The King of Kings has arrived,
The choice is yours to decide,

I urge all humans to bury their pride,
To manifest the spiritual jewels that are locked away inside.

Upon your humbleness, My Heavenly Father shall appear,
Reach deep into your heart, as God and I are always near.

For he is you, and you are he,
He's the big picture, for we are the key.

I shall comfort those who mourn,
As I offer them a chance to be Spiritually reborn.

I merely come to Conquer and fulfill,
As I offer many human cups, a Spiritual refill.

Everyone shall drink from my Spiritual straw,
The narrowness defines God's Superiority Law.

Everyone shall grab a hold of their flaws, then
Give it to God for the ultimate Spiritual Thaw.

My Heavenly Father is Spiritually real,
Please believe as this is a huge ordeal.

I shall allow many humans to Spiritually see and eternally feel,
As I, the Lamb of God, am offering everyone a chance to,
"Heal with Neal."

Neal is my last name; please adhere as I have come to proclaim.
I am the Son of the Living God,

I have returned; what were the odds?

Do not be afraid, For I am Heavenly made.

I extend my Spiritual cup to everyone and offer a worldly trade,
Do not mind COVID, for I am Spiritually and Heavenly sprayed.

The cup, which symbolizes my blood,
Shall cleanse you like Noah's flood.

The time is here,
Please stand by as the new Jerusalem appears.

Change is commanded within your heart,
As the only way to see the new Jerusalem is with a Spiritual Spark.

I am the way, the truth, and God's light,
Please refill your cups and prepare for this Spiritual fight.

Give me your sins, and I shall give them away,
My Heavenly Father is waiting to hear from every child right away.

Upon your trade, God himself shall invade,
Which allows the creator to renew your mind, body and soul, just as a saved
child has prayed.

2

SPIRITUAL TOUCHDOWN POEM!

Ask me where I have been, and I shall show you,
The truth is held within my testimony,
Attached to the worldly things that humans go through.

After exposing lies comes the truth,
I am the black messiah, and here is my inner enlightened proof,

Wool-like hair,
Upon taking my Police oath, my face was bare,

One like the son of Man,
Entails I AM part human,

Hair as white as snow,
Entails the 7 Spiritual gifts and ultimate wisdom that my Heavenly Father bestows,
Hair like wool entails my tangled black mane,
Inhaling the Tree of Life explains my eye's red flame.

Feet like fine brass,

Too, explains my dark hue skin, herb of the field, and the Tree for Life, which
is the marijuana-seeded grass.

Nothing is by mistake,
It was meant to be this way,

"Yall gon learn today."

How that false image of a light hue Jesus,
Caused such an abandoning dark disarray.

For those who don't believe,
Reevaluate your heart as I have been delivered for thy Holy heart,
Within the rebirth of the righteous shall I retrieve
The man behind the hidden heart,
I was once a Police Officer,
As I took an oath and delivered on my part.

Always remember, blessed are the peacemakers,
Upon my flesh signing, did my journey end with a Spiritual spark.

A spark of deceit from my employing agency,
Tons of anger from those who did not understand,
Those who played a role in said deceit and ill-will shall feel God's wrath,
As the Holy Spirit has touchdown on earth, within the wicked shall my Heav-
enly Father eternally reprimand.

3

WHO AM I! - POEM

Church in Lake Placid, Florida

If you have no clue,
Bow Down as I introduce myself to you.
I am greater than Father Abraham, Isaac, and Jacob simply because I inherit
their combined spiritual makeup.

Check out my tattoos, it's a Spiritual thing,
Reviewing my tattoos reveals my enlightened spiritual wings.

My heart is as beautiful as a butterfly,
Open your heart unto mine, and you shall see with God's vision, and here
is why.

I sit at the height of your emotion, carried unto your feet, Many humans only
pray in my name when they feel worldly weak.

I also guide the meek, all while using my Heavenly Father's Spiritual
technique.

Who AM I?

Take a look into my heart as I offer a sneak peek,
Unto my peak is where you and God shall meet.

Inside my heart is where heaven resides; I shall guide all those who divinely
and whole heartedly abide.

I pray all is well,

Without one's wholeness unto themselves,
It's impossible to provide my blood to your cells.

The flow of my righteous blood through your veins, Shall place you within my
spiritual lane, Along my Heavenly Father's Spiritual plane.

Who Am I?

I woke up like this,
Revealing the truth like stored away treasure,

A hint unto my Spiritual existence is,
I once slept through a storm, which bared stormy weather.

I really love lions, which signifies my pride, Judah is my home; I belong to
their Holy tribe.

Who AM I?

I will provide one more hint,
Which entails a slow walk, not a sprint.
I am the True King, that every human shall walk like,
I left my Bible blueprint for every human to mimic, which sheds Heavenly
insight.

Who AM I?

Hold your breath; please do not Spiritually choke,
I shall offer you sight beyond your eyes, for you shall become Spiritually
woke.

How is this for Spiritual reality, I AM your Lord, who has been sent by God,
My entire thinking can be summed up by Godly Moses and his God-given Rod.

I am the Messiah, and my Angels multiply like grains of sand, I am the lamb of
God, sent to deliver on God's foretold plan.

The journey will be shown by displaying the sight within me; I am the author
and the finisher, The one who holds the key.

See with your heart, in order to be free,
I am the Hebrew King; I hold the highest Spiritual God-delivered Degree.

Do you recognize my inner image, or can I not be seen,
It must be that false image, that foolish men created of me, Even after God
advised not to intervene.

Yet, as a black man, I shall soar,

For I bore eagles' wings, as I love my Heavenly Father, from the depths of my
seeking core,
Knock, knock, knock,
Guess who's at your door?

It's the Hebrew King, for we shall all gather many things,
Like our exile before, I pray everyone has prepared for this Spiritual war.

4

HEAVENLY DISORDER POEM

Heaven is everything you can imagine, But not what you think.
This message is for the masses, the ones Connected by the Spiritual link.

As God winks, he allows for a spiritual blink,
Which commands all humans to sip from my Spiritual drink.
Heaven is stored within your heart and mind, Many shall see, even the blind.

Changing your thinking shall save your life, have faith like Father Abraham as he grabbed that knife.

God commanded him to sacrifice his son.
little did he know, once he grabbed the knife, his sacrifice was done.

A ram saved the day, but only after Father Abraham raised his knife to obey.

We shall all blink away our sins,
Which entails provisions from a well-known friend.

His name is Jesus, and he resides within me,
I am Jesus in the flesh, as my heart and mind are soaring Heavenly free.

The Holy Ghost is my interior force,
The Holy Bible speaks on my return, which is the ultimate blue printed source.

We are all Kings, but I am at the top,
My Heavenly Father sits above me, but we all are the cream of the crop.

If you are smart, you shall see how a man displays Love from the depths of his inner heart.

As Judah means praise, cheer openly without shame,
For the Lion from the tribe of Judah has returned to ignite your Spiritual flame.

God's revolution has started; I urge all to believe,
I am the one true prophet sent to place thy hearts at ease.

Free your mind, as God demands control,
I Am the key of David; place my thoughts within thy keyhole.

The hole is thy heart; with entry, it shall offer you a fresh start, By placing your mind off the Worldly chart.

Then comes the Spiritual Realm, which is what we control, We imply God and me, as I have come to fulfill the foretold.

As a man thinketh in his heart, so is he,
I urge all humans to reach deep into their hearts,
To pull out the best version of them, which is also the Spiritual version of me.

The kingdom does not come with observation,
It's within you programmed on God's spiritual station.
Let's all heal as a nation and spread joy,
Celebrating the return of the King, who landed with a bellboy.

Blare your horns; blare them loud and proud,

Say it with me: JESUS HAS RETURNED!

Why not say it aloud?

I am your Lord; spiritually, hop aboard.
In other words, I am the Messiah, and there is only one who sits higher,

He is the spirit of Love, which encompasses every heart,
Please think of me as the second Noah, the chosen one who began Earth's restart.

Citations:

Luke 17:20-21 (*Jesus Spoken Words.......*)

"The kingdom of God does not come with observation;

nor will they say, "See here!" or "See there!" For indeed, the The Kingdom of God is within you."

5

THORNED TRUTH POEM

As I lie on the sloped surface, with
Sticks in my back,
The ground is killing me,
It must be my melanated skin,
I doubt it's hurting because I am black.

The sense of confusion is that racism still exists,
The thorns are now placed on our wages,
Rather than iron shackles on our feet and wrist
I must remain humble,
To refrain from that awkward stumble,
The one where if you miss a step,
Your Spiritual walk will crumble,

Causing the inner voice of God to become distance and mumbled.

God has chosen me to shed light on what is,
Just like the test within the world,
I shall offer all a Spiritual quiz.

Do you believe in my Heavenly Father, who you can't see?
Do you genuinely believe that the majority of black people are free?
Do you believe you are created in the image of God?

Or are you one of those people who solely believe in the Big Bang Theory,
Which assumes humans are a product of a natural disaster and my Heavenly
Father is a fraud,
And also feels that this whole Spiritual world is a façade.

Do you accept your godly power?
Which allows you to sit at God's right hand,
Bridging the connection between the tower and the stand,
Also known as the Spiritual Body and the Tangible Man.

Do you believe Heaven resides within your heart?
Or are you waiting for a physical Heaven to begin doing your part?
Do you believe Heaven is a place for your eyes to behold?
Or is Heaven a place attached to the hidden heart,
For a worldly human to unfold.

Do you believe God has delivered on his promise?
Do you believe Jesus Christ has returned and is walking among us?
What color do you think he would be?
Would you believe me if I told you he was me? Markais Ruben. C Neal Sr
For I am all I can be,
I am God, and God is Me,
I AM the chosen one,
Also known as his Spiritual mini-me.

Blare your horns as the time is here,
I can no longer lie on the ground,
Despite the thorns, my Heavenly Father has commanded me to appear.

I often pray to my Heavenly Father, begging him to return home,
The world is filled with many judas', betraying each other,
Just as they did the spirit the first time back in Rome.

6

SPIRITUAL SCRATCH POEM

I Have a Spiritual itch that's hard to reach,
Heaven is open, for I am the earth's Heavenly Breach
The gates are forced open by a Man of God,
I shall ram many doors, using God's Spiritual "Taurus" Rod
Although I have forced entry, please welcome me in,
I shall scratch your Spiritual itch, which bears no worldly sin.

Upon ramming your door, if there's no damage created,
We are Spiritually related; as a believer, you have awaited.

If your door bears damage, there are sins you must manage,
Scratch away and leave marks, which shall cause spiritual sparks, unto your once tainted heart.

I possess the Holy Spirit of Love, which flows like many seas,
Humans must get a hold of their itch, which is like a dead dog dying from fleas.

Every unrighteous choice has an adverse effect,
Within thy ill will decisions shall God's Holy Spirit detect

The deep itch saddens my redeeming soul;
Humans are rejecting their Spiritual power, implying that the Spiritual Scratch's power is getting out of control.

Let the truth be told: the dogs are the foolish boys,
Which bear fleas that society can't control.

They are dead and dying as they honor their flesh,
Absent of the Holy Spirit, as their Spiritual Scratch is their ultimate human test.

Within thy Spiritual Scratch, within thy Spiritual stroke,
Please rub and irritate all unrighteousness within thy heart to regain my Heavenly Father's Spiritual Yoke.

Within Yahweh's loving hand, which allows a human to Spiritually see,
Rejecting God's loving power is like a termite-infested decaying house tree.

The wooden house is a human vessel, and the tree can be seen as a symbol of life,

The termites are the forever unrighteous humans who deny Jesus, As I have returned, again paying the ultimate price.

Men operate on logic, and women on emotion,
You both shall uplift one another, as together, you define God's Spiritual motion.

Satisfy your scratch, by stepping away from sin, Spiritually rebirth yourselves;
Heavenly it's the only way to get in.

Reach deep into your heart, followed by your mind, Please take your time, as I am challenging to find.

I am your Lord; I am your greatest supporter, Spiritually scratch away all your sins,

God first, then I, in that exact order.

I am God, as we are one,
I am Markais Ruben. C Neal Sr, his "Only Begotten Son."

If thy Scratch is overlooked, a considerable hindrance it shall be,
Please claw and scratch away all sin, which bears Spiritual wisdom and divine
knowledge unto me.

Within the healing faith of thy scar that the scratching has made,
Sweet glory when one manifests Spiritual gifts from overcoming their wrongdoings, having no ill Intentions, or being unrighteously swayed.

Within the irritation of thy itch, all shall pray for Spiritual revelation and
freedom,
To those who are Holy sanctified, unto the righteous and unrighteous, has Jesus
returned to Heavenly and Holy redeem God's gems.

Acknowledge God's power, and all shall be forgiven; I AM God's son, who
stands atop of Spirituality, even above the partition of earthly religion.

Spiritually scratching defines worldly decay,
Denying of thy flesh and entering Heaven along the merry way.

As Heaven is not tangibly here or there, it is within thy heart, Standing firm as
the General Sherman tree,
As your God has returned for the righteously tall, upward bounding start.

7
____

SPIRITUAL DECLUTTER

Given the time is at hand, all humans shall remove all clutter from their hearts and minds. Clutter can be summed up as any one of the Seven Deadly Sins and anything that distracts your love from the love of my Heavenly Father.

The Seven Deadly Sins are self-explanatory, as they are recognizable in the hearts of the sinners. All those who sin have dimmed lights simply due to their disobedience, and when they are in the presence of two or more, their dimmed light emits high frequency for God's chosen children, which is undisguised.

When two or more tainted Spirits, disguised as humans, gather, they speak from the tip of their eroded heart, which is opposite from the depths of where my Heavenly Father resides. The opposite can be displayed as the human will speak opposite from the "Fruits of the Heart." Their conversation bears ill feelings and can cause hate-driven emotions. Their pleasure of gossip reigns as they go from human to human and speak ill on their names, which govern their life. Their motives to deceive others can be driven by jealousy or lack of their own pride, as stealing a human's belongings manifests laziness as the ability to work hard has been applied to a worldly bum.

The bum reference can be applied to any human who lurks in the shadows to prey on another human who can or cannot defend themselves. So essentially, a person with poor, harmful, or wrong qualities that preys on the weak far too often, as one time is too many in the Spiritual sights of my Heavenly Father.

Human Shadow lurking is ill-advised, while Spiritual Shadow lurking is left up to my Heavenly Father. One implies ill will, while the other signifies a manifestation of light that has surfaced from the face of the deep.

The manifestation is allowing God, while the light is a human seeing with God's vision. The surface from the face of the deep implies a human being fully adhering to God's power as their thoughts and actions shall be displayed on the earth's surface. In essence, it's when a human offers their Spiritual light unto all others, even those with a dimmed light.

Spiritual Shadow lurking is when my Heavenly Father, who operates in the Spirit, devours dark souls as his prey is a wrongdoer. My Heavenly Father is the light that brightens my morning star. Our light shall illuminate the human body, which appears bright amongst the dark world. The light, which consumes any darkness, can be observed by the Spiritual rays a human emits when their tongue is governed by the nine fruits of the heart.

The only two entities that can operate within the shadows are the two spirits themselves, The Holy Spirit and the Holy Spirit's adversary. A Human being shall not operate within the shadows as their lack of Spiritual sight within the darkness shall further the lost tribes of Israel, as when one tribe member becomes lost, is not the whole tribe lost?

The Holy Spirit despises the serpent, which is his adversary. Given God created all there is to create, including the cunning disguise of the serpent, he, being the All-Mighty, can operate on any portion of any side, as his creation exists within all things. Furthermore, my Heavenly Father has total control, which means any other perceived control from man or false Gods is just an imitation of what my Heavenly Father actually is.

The Holy Spirit operates off love and seeks to destroy the darkness from opposite spirits. God's love is made perfect as he governs and delivers the Holy Spirit.

Suppose a human's life is filled with clutter. In that case, they will have difficulty hearing my Heavenly Father as he constantly attempts to deliver the Holy Spirit to his hopeful, obedient children.

Many are called, and a few are chosen; the selection lies within a human's choices, while the call is placed on every human with a heart and mind. The few signify my Heavenly Father's sadness as many reject his Godly power, which allows them to operate within his frequency, allowing a mere human to be created in the image of God. Male or female, as God implies man and Goddess implies female. The creation allows the human, of flesh, to operate within God's Spirit, which sits within the firmament, where a mere human has dared to reach (2 Timothy 3).

The time has come for all mere humans to reach the depths of their hearts and allow God to resurface from the face of the deep. The Spiritual awakening shall place their mere human thoughts underneath the thoughts of my Heavenly Father's many words. The control the world seeks towards human understanding shall be matched up against the inner standing of God, as I, being his only begotten son, have come to offer the world clarity.

8

SPIRITUAL DECLUTTER POEM

Reveal God's face as you open your heart.
Manifest God's power by doing your part.

Take a step out of the dark, which urges no wrong,
Adhere to God's commandments, given to Moses, engraved in stone.

Declutter your thoughts and make way for the new,
take a step back and bow down as I reveal myself to you.

I am the Host of the Spirits, inhabited by man,
God has blessed me with being the beginning to the world's new plans.

Do not fret, for I have come to make all things new,
Come be with me, as God wants you at his right hand, too.

As Moses advised, let my people go,
The King of Kings has arrived to share my eternal glow.

The reign is mine, as the gates to heaven are open, Come feast with me, as I
have come to guide the broken.

I will walk you through the pearly gates, one step at a time,
But you must adhere to my Holy words, as they are Spiritually and truly divine.

I am your Lord; cleanse your hearts and hop aboard.

Please do not hoard,
Declutter all your burdens as they are not yours.

9

SPIRITUAL EYE POEM

Buckingham Royal Palace- London, United Kingdom.

My image is disguised by the silhouette which hides,
The Holy Spirit, which God has delivered for humans to thrive.

I am here to gather all those that matter,
I shall be your ladder, which bears high-frequency uplifting chatter.

You shall climb aboard without fear,
No worries, Our Heavenly Father has sent me here.

I am a blessing to anyone who is stressing,
It would be best if you willfully offered your confession, which involves
releasing your transgressions.
The human heart must be clear for my love to appear; God is the spirit of love,
which makes my fleshly image unclear.

The Tree of Life resides within the midst of the herbs,
The once-forbidden tree, my Heavenly Father advised the man not to disturb.

The cannabis smoke, which symbolizes dust of the ground, As man inhales, he
travels and becomes spiritually bound.

The leap which comes after inhaling through your nostrils, seek the love of
God, which shall erase all things hostel.

Breathe in and out while taking one step at a time, Please be careful, as I will
guide your eternal Spiritual climb.

The ladder, which no man can see, resides within my heart, So, what's with all
the false images of me.

I have dark hue skin, as if burned in a furnace, I have come to claim my throne,
That the world has tarnished.

I am King of all Kings, sitting above all humans,
I am Half man, Half God, which makes me Spiritually Superhuman.

I am no better than anymore, for we are all the same,
I have made my choice, thank you for praying in my name.

I AM, Jesus Christ, in the flesh of man; please do not shut down, For I have
just began.

I have returned to restore world order,
Would you like me to wait, while you get your life in order?

I will do no such thing as the time is here. Do you Remember my last words, I advised all that I was near.

I said,
"Surely I am coming Quickly."

For quickly I have come, brace for impact as I have come to clean the earthly scum.

My Heavenly Father has delivered on his promise, By placing the Holy Spirit back into man,
I have the ultimate power, known as a Spiritual scan.

The time is now, please do not make God in the flesh wait,
Reach into the depths of your heart and allow my Heavenly Father and I, to carry your burdened weight.

10

SPIRITUAL TIMETABLE

Jerusalem Israel

Time is of the essence; time is one of the greatest gifts,

within God's timely lift-off,

Shall all his angels resurrect from their worldly graveyard shift

Spiritual time does not come with a clock; it is more like a Spiritual meter,

Within the hearts of the unrighteous, shall their hearts be scorched With fire, Implying within a furnace, like a massive unbearable heater.

Within a righteous heart which is filled with Gold and Silver,

Unto their Ankh rebirth, shall their Holy River flow, allowing Yahweh to openly deliver.

Surrounding thy faithful truth, which shall encompass their whole heart,

Unto God's Heavenly spark shall a human be exalted into the Likeness of Noah's lifesaving ark

Within thy worldly time, within God's Spiritual heightened measures,

Unto thy meter of truth, shall God's love soar, making all things new, Which were created for thy loveable pleasure.

Within God's gopherwood, within the rebuild for a righteous life,

Unto my carpenter lifestyle, has the Holy Spirit come, erecting all Things Holy for the righteous afterlife.

All sins shall be accounted for as they are placed on God's Holy table,

Throughout a human's time on earth, shall they offer their sins,

Is thy spirit of unrighteous Cain or of righteous Abel?

Unto God's Spiritual Timetable, unto the table of time,

I AM the Lamb of God, offering all my sheep a Heavenly chance to Flock back into God's Holy line.

Even upon thy own Spiritual time,

Shall all Righteousness manifest, rewind, implying bringing all Things back to thy mind

God advised the expectancy of Heaven was sure to come,

Imploring for mercy on thy soul, Adding together all things, thereby Totaling their righteous sum.

Place all things done onto the scale of justice,

Pray thy heart is light as a feather, Spiritually implying the Holy diet Of an animal known as a wooly-haired cuscus.

What does your inner heart hold upon thy fruit-bearing seed and Upon the bearing of thy own fruit?

What defiles a human is what comes from the depths of their heart, Upon thy thoughts and dialogue uproot.

Upon thy Spiritual calling, how can one lose,

Only by remaining asleep, rejecting even thy own power, eternal Damnation as thy heart continues to hit that Spiritual snooze.

Many humans have missed my Heavenly Father's calling by Purposely wanting to sleep,

Spiritual Timetable, I AM, Jesus Christ,

It's Spiritual time to awaken and stop playing within the world's Darkened deceit.

I have Spiritually come to claim my worldly throne; within the Perfection of Heaven shall I tune in and hone.

Seeking solely truth and endless joy on my path, within God's Spiritual Timetable, is faith Solitude, Implying an alone, isolated bath.

Sprinkling showers of midstful gifts, one tear at a time, bringing back All unrighteousness, within the passing by of God's whiffle remind.

Into the testament of truth shall the glory unfold. Removing the wool From thy eyes, too, implies removing thy earthly blindfold.

Upon removal, the time shall move peculiar and Spiritually strange,

Heaven parallels earth, time to swap places, unto denying thy flesh For God's love in exchange.

Total Healing-Faith opportunity, wholeness within the paradigm of Heaven,

Mirror opposite of thy worldly, flesh-driven oppression.

Sad discernment that rages war on love, some are Godless children, Implying they deny my Heavenly Father Yahweh, and I, Jesus Christ, Who has risen from above.

Into the world, I have been delivered, in the perfect timing of God's Morning star,

I AM the 7th child, and upon God's calling, we want you just the way you are.

Applying acknowledgment unto Christ and a willing nature to change,

Into the hearts of the chosen, should they have felt God's presence Was to be close and within range.

Within thy meter or time, within thy time or meter,

Within the height of thy righteous deeds, within thy recognition of God's Spiritual majority leader

At the top of the class among my Spiritual sheep, within the love of my brothers and sisters, for within their Healing Faith shall I forever seek.

God's timetable has arrived; please place all sins on thy worldly table,

Hoarding of any truth shall be detected and at all cost be Spiritually fatal.

Healing-Faith.org

11

INNER GLOW POEM

I am a star that glees on demand, mimicking the Sirius star
Known as the brightest star placed in the skies above the land.

For all things I shall withstand, as my Heavenly Father has delivered the spirit
unto me to fulfill and expand, I pray for every human to understand.

My Supernova shine, makes up God's interior Spiritual design, as his love
encourages soughtful treasures, which all humans Shall desire to find.

My dark Hue bears understanding to the man standing in my shoes.

My Spiritual Hue connects the breakthrough that allows God's foretold views,
Just remain true as God's love passes through,
which shall shed unto all things which are made Heavenly new.

Here is a preview,
See with your heart and not your eyes, rely on the love of God, To resurrect the
inner shine from inside.

All shall abide, for all those who decide,

Drop your pride, which manifests a supernova light, as your guide.

Strike the match and light the path beneath your feet,
Please pick up your cross, known as burdens, and follow after me.

I shall offer sight beyond what you can see,
It involves interior visions, from your inner man unto me,

The inner man is known as your mini-me,
But Spiritually, the entire picture is more significant than just you
and me.

As we all shall pray to foresee, doing so shall illuminate you as the perfect
candidate or nominee.

Plant thy seed, and watch how it grows,
Please prepare for your overflow, as my Heavenly Father has Spiritual wisdom
to bestow.

Open your Spiritual heart and not your worldly eyes,
If you are led by sight, you will miss One hell of a Heavenly surprise.

I Am God, and I offer a trade, It's more like a gift I shall give, As I am Heav-
enly Made,
Please do not be afraid; I am the Hebrew King, Who shall guide this Spiritual
Crusade.
My Father advised, let there be light, and there it was,
All because the love for his children soared well above
Above all other things,
As humans are his greatest creation,
We shall all praise and sing,
As the Holy spirit, has made it to my destination.

Read Psalms, remain and sustain,
As the Spiritual firmament is my Aim.

Unshackled by all shame, take ownership of your sins, as we all shall realize there is no one else to blame.

Everything happens for a reason, Denying me as the Son of Man, is known as Spiritual Treason,
It's a Spiritual meaning coupled with the Spiritual Season,
Please do not make excuses, as my Heavenly Father and I shall bypass all foolish reasons.

Rejoice for the return of the Hebrew King, As God has seen my light, that it is good.

Deny yourself and follow me,
To be all Spiritual, implying, mentally, emotionally, and physically understood.

First were the Hebrews, then the Israelites, and Now the Blacks, Thank God I am back; I am Christ the Second coming,
Excuse me as I use my inner Spiritual light to unpack.

BLACK BEAUTY POEM

Martin Luther King Jr Memorial - Washington, D.C "OUT OF THE MOUNTAIN OF DESPAIR, A STONE OF HOPE."

Building up one race does not mean tearing down others,
I am the Hebrew king, sent to liberate all humans, especially my people of color.

Here is my Plea: for the blacks to indeed be free,
Give them money and land, just as America gave the Indians when they came with their demands.

Here I stand, 405 slavery years later; Jesus has returned, and I have been sent by the world's creator.

You cannot enslave an entire race, force them to build up your world, and then tell them they are out of place.

The hate coupled with anger is out of control,
The blacks are the beacons; it's time we play our Spiritual roles, Which shall manifest the story to unfold.

As a whole, we are affixed to God at the depths of our souls,
Our ultimate goal is to conquer the Heavenly promised land, as the Holy Bible foretold.

Just as the movie avatar, we are the key,

The power is within our hearts, attached to God's Spiritual decree,
To obtain the Spiritual power, you must first agree,
To follow Jesus Christ, as my love shall set thy Heavenly heart free.

Step away from the segregation and the pain, My black brothers and sisters,
you are gods, Within the Spiritual plane.

I have come in the flesh;
To unchain all humans upon my Heavenly Father's request.

Although we are all blessed, the earth is a mess,
Therefore, I shall provide the ultimate test, which shall free the hearts and
minds of the oppressed.

If all people are equal, why are blacks last?
Could it be because of our anger, developed by America's treatment in the past?
It's quite the contrast.

Blacks are frustrated because we deserve more, Our death tolls are too high for
anyone to ignore.

Give the blacks reparations and watch their quality of life grow.
Is that why we've been suppressed all these years? Because the blacks possess
the eternal glow?

13

—————

BROTHERLY LOVE POEM

I get torn down by my race like no other,
It helps me realize that a beloved brother doesn't associate by pigmented color.

Dark Hue is my skin, with the inner God from within, If your words are unkind to me,
you clearly don't know where I've been, Nor from whom I descend,
As I spin the block for another go, I am Christ, the second coming, to provide Spiritual dough.

Other blacks make me feel so low, Having the mentality of a Jim Crow,
But for why, though?
All those hateful things men and women must forgo.
Hair as white as snow,
Rains down wisdom for my heart and mind to show.

I come in Peace, although I am a former Police.

I come to provide a glimpse into heaven,
Guess what number child I am? That's right, Number Seven.

I have come to break leaven, with those who pray in my name,
I have come to heal the sick, the ones who the world calls mentally insane.

The ones who believe in something they can not see, but yet they know exist,
The ones who say the words, I pray, as opposed to the words, I wish.

The bread, which symbolizes my body, combines my blood with the wine, For together, we are embodied.

I am God's only begotten son,
And I shall set everyone free.

Are you a tree that bears good fruit, Or are you rotten to the worst degree?

The only way to see is through I, the son, My resurrection date was 9/22/2021,

So technically, I have just begun.
Those who openly deny me will be sorry, Upon their attempts to enter the pearly gates,
It will be like a child being late or absent for school, known as an unexcused absent or tardy.

You may not enter, Unless I grant permission,
I AM the Messiah, who shall guide this Spiritual expedition, But here are a few provisions.

Be kind to everyone you meet, And live life with a Heavenly spark.

Test those Spirits,
which are spoken by the nine fruits of the heart.

If my Heavenly Father resides there, I have faith he will show.
Voice as the sound of many waters, Have a dialogue and watch how it go.

Remember, God is love, whereas the devil is hate.

Speaking badly about other humans,
Reveal your inner heart, which carries burden-Weight, but don't seal your own fate.

By manifesting self-hate,
Always remember,
My Heavenly Father makes no mistakes.

Just as Manna was a collection of bread, and Rest on the seventh day.

I am the lamb of God,
Who has Heavenly come from far, far away!

14

THE STOIC OF BEING SAVED!

Mount Quarantania/Mount of Temptation/ Jebel Quruntul Israeli-occupied
West Bank, State of Palestine

Being saved means upon the return of Jesus Christ, you will not deny the Host; any man who lies upon making foolish allegations of being the Almighty deserves every wrath to lash. The Holy Bible advises all to test the Spirit by the Spirit.

One must believe in the entire Bible, not just bits and pieces, as some religious groups will have you believe.

You must believe in the Father, the Son, and the Holy Spirit. Just as every prophet is a gift from God, you, too, must believe in the Prophet of Jesus Christ! The fact remains that no one will know the day, time, hour, or image of Jesus Christ upon said return. Not even your Pastor or Pope shall know. So, any man who says they have seen GOD's face is a lie. Along with that lie comes the Seven Deadly Sins disguised in the midst of pleasant things treasured by man. (***Exodus 33:12-22***)

God is a Spirit, not an image. The Spirit can reside within humans, but it is a stand-alone entity of God; it must be housed within a living organism to operate. The correlation, too, shall parallel when my Heavenly Father advised all not to create or idolize false images. ***(Leviticus 19:4).*** Do you recall when Moses became angry regarding the Golden Calf Statue ***Exodus 32***

Be more Spiritual, less religious, as religion attaches notions to things that the Holy Bible does not say. Many religions hold perceptions from humans, which sometimes causes false condemnation, as someone reading between the lines to draw out their conclusion is still a human, assuming what my Heavenly Father meant. Spirituality takes you higher than any other entity, as God has no boundaries and operates in the Spirit.

1.) Many will deny Jesus upon his return, given his preconceived image compared to the selected Host's appearance, given the false images which are and were created. Why did Dark Hue skin become Light Hue when creating an ill-advised image of me? Jesus!

2.) Many will say to themselves, "Am I ready for the judgment day?" How can it be? But I thought. Is he really black? God wouldn't choose a past sinner, would he? Has God really delivered his promise to the world by allowing his only begotten Son, Jesus Christ! to return to the earth's Realm?

I, Markais Ruben. C Neal Sr, I am the Host of the spirits; I shall and will assure you that no matter what question you may have, I am indeed the Hebrew child sent by God. I have come to conquer World Peace. I, too, have come to free the hearts and minds of all the humans who believe in my Heavenly Father and his highly anticipated promise of, I, Jesus Christ resurrecting.

Has anyone lived according to God's will, or have They lived according to their own will?

Do they complain about the cards God dealt them, or do they attempt to seek understanding towards those cards? There is an enormous difference.

The difference describes a human complaining about their deck of cards, which hinders growth, while the other human attempts to understand why those cards are chosen throughout the deck, which bears an urge for growth—the why must be implied unto oneself, as their understanding is meant for them.

The irony is that every human has control of their mind and heart, which is required for a human to bear life on earth. So, with the love of God, which is thy heart, combined with the conscious/woke mind, which derives the human choice, all shall gather the courage to face their fear of my Heavenly Father, which consists of having blind faith.

Being Spiritually blind allows the controller of the Spiritual Realm, God, to have sights on his obedient child. The child without a vision for sin shall only see through the eyes of the inner man, known as Jesus. The new perception from the Spiritual King offers a new look into discernment from God as opposed to man *(__John 9:35-39__)*.

__John 9:39__

And Jesus said, "For judgment, I have come into this world, that those who do not see may see, and that those who see may be made blind."

3.) Many will ponder on the thought of Jesus being Black. - Dark Hue skin, hair like wool, a carpenter (which signifies his profession and ability to absorb such heat (rich in melanin pigment), Often referred to as "Black People.

4.) Many will deny my arrival, given they are living by their own will and rules as opposed to my Heavenly Father's will and the rules within the book of life, the Holy Bible.

5.) Many will deny my arrival, given the thoughts of others, if they believe in such a claim. I will assure you this: believing in my Heavenly Father, whom you cannot see, is crazy, yet he exists! Just as denying his only begotten Son, whom you can see, is too crazy. Yet it's true.

I am the "Messiah" whom every prophet spoke about. I am the "King of Peace" who has come to restore world order. I am the "Redeemer" who shall open the door to any human who knocks, as I offer the "Bread of Life" as "I Am" the "Holy One of Israel."

The gates of Heaven are open to stoic followers of my Heavenly Father and I.

15

SPIRITUAL EXTRACTION OF TRAUMA

Within the Earth realm, I've learned that many traumas are through each person's experiences rather than a generational one.

The longer a person lives will determine their level of accumulated trauma. If a person dies prematurely, then their trauma ends at death. When a person is living in the flesh and is dead at heart, their trauma too will soon end in death if they don't begin to act swiftly unto the Holy Spirit, which is attached to everyone's inner acknowledging heart.

I have learned that drugs are merely a coping mechanism, not a cause of mental Illness. Those subjected to consuming drugs are attempting to mass a much bigger problem, the problem of life. The problem of life means specific events within their lives have caused them to hold on to a form of emotion other than Love and Peace, as God promised his children.

Traumatizing events have degrees of injuries, meaning the worse events lead to many other smaller events. If a person has a childhood trauma that was over-looked or forced to be concealed, their paradigm is reconstructed from that point forward as they were made to make sense of something that doesn't. Their influential minds unknowingly or knowingly remember trauma because of the lack of sense it made, suppressing their mind and heart or a form of guilt or attention.

They can only move forward in the spirit once specific events are addressed in their minds. Furthermore, addressing the situation does not mean merely speaking about the traumatic event; it also means shedding light on the wrong that was done, especially if that wrong can set another soul free from trauma. The earth calls this "closed mouth don't get fed," but it's

called foolishness within the spirit. How can someone pray unto my Heavenly Father for the release of trauma if said trauma holds connections to other people's trauma? If everyone blares their horns (dialogue) and becomes an adult in many situations, mental health will cease as the truth will set everyone free.

No more attempting to link all mental illnesses to generational issues, meaning focusing so much on their family issues and begin diving into their exclusive traumatic events, one by one; once you work your way through said trauma, then childhood trauma should follow unless that childhood trauma is the biggest hindrance. Then, allow the heart to be healed as it wishes, meaning allow the trauma to unfold but one event at a time, as exposure to trauma brings fatigue and exhaustion to the mind and body.

Placing our Heavenly Father above all and allowing people to open their hearts and speak about their situations is the only way to heal them genuinely. The medication suppresses or creates emotional disregulation of feelings that will eventually be unleashed. Just as the medication is temporary, so are traumatizing events.

Here is the top reason for mental illness.

Suppression in any form, whether of the mind or financial, forces a person to remain in the world, spiritually, for a lot longer than our Heavenly Father intended. If God is Love and we were created in his image, male and female, wouldn't that mean once a person reaches a certain level of peace, their heart radiates Love for all people, not only unto themselves? Once that form of Grace from God happens, that person shall become a cheerful giver of unconditional Love and forgiveness; as God's grace was shown to them, it shall be reciprocated.

While holding in things from that past, a few complex emotions that can surface are anger, confusion, and resentment. The level of said emotions is determined by the degree of the traumatic incident within their minds that is causing mental illness-like behavior.

Most people hold the trauma through their own experiences alone and no one else; this means their trauma is not linked to their parents in any way, shape, or form. These are called isolated traumatic events. Several events can be discovered and managed with proper extraction techniques. A proper technique is reaching their hearts with comfort and care while discerning through their broken memory clips as it acts like a movie among their remembrance. Dissect each traumatic event and its entirety before moving to the next traumatizing event. If done improperly, the trauma will not cease but could merely manifest into unusual dysfunctional emotions.

The type of Trauma linked to a child's upbringing holds massive weight, as their childhood sponge days could bore many horrid events. These events can be considered a generational curse. Such as racism, anger, sexual immortality, confusion, or worse, if they were being led away from God.

Prayerfully, Our Heavenly Father graced us with the Holy Bible and two parents as a guide, but if one or both parents have been led away from God, how can proper teachings ever occur? That means only the Bible and God's chosen children remain for a hopeful tutor.

Racism is a taught behavior as it sees color as a sign of filth rather than a Godly jewel. Or it sees dark hue as a sign of weakness rather than being looked at as a tainted gold star that once was bronze. The faintness comes from minor discoloration, which compares to the trials and tribulations of the black community today.

Anger can only be transferred, not created, such as energy. If a person holds manifested hate within their hearts from childhood, then their anger is not theirs to carry. It was merely transferred anger from the ill teachings of their parents and peers, or being totally misguided altogether as them not being shown God's grace through the teachings of their parents, has caused an enormous barrier between thy seed and her seed. Anger is also caused by specific events shaping a person's paradigm. Substances can enhance the development of anger, but anger is not born within our hearts, which indicates a cause-and-effect chain.

The cause is what event or reason transpired which caused the "Hippocampus" to remember and display such behavior. The Hippocampus is linked to the cerebral cortex, which is associated with our highest mental capabilities. The cerebral cortex can be divided into three functional areas: Primary (Motor), Secondary (Sensory), and Associative. Essentially, it is linked to learning and memory, among other things. A specific event can alter one's mind, as can the proper extraction technique.

The effect is the ill outcomes derived from the causes. But only the host of said Trauma can blare their horns to be heard by God's angels, who hold many spiritual jewels, one being a righteous counselor.

Only until Mental Health is understood to be a problem of the world and not of God will proper teaching begin on how to take the Mental Health community by storm.

God promised Love for all his children. Mental Health is a way for God to reach those who cry for help. The submission of the cries shall not be dealt with by suppressing said people with pharmaceutical drugs, which are linked to millions of horrid stories given their chemical mixture. The most feasible approach thus far is " The Holistic Approach," which was introduced in 1975. The Spiritual portion is what I'm amazed by.

Medical Marijuana is also a great way to help treat mental Illness. The more natural, God-given "Tree of Life" plant, as opposed to a mixture of chemicals that Man deems safe even after all the reported destruction that many prescription medications have brought.

My testimony firsthand can bring credence to the possible destruction pharmaceutical drugs can bring. I have tried nearly 15 different types of medications with hopes of releasing trauma, only to realize once I acknowledged the origin of my trauma.

God was my only source, as he guided me towards the herbs of the field, which were created on the third day, not toward man, who was created on the sixth day.

16

CLOUDED SPIRITUAL TRAVELS!

Saints Sergius and Bacchus Church Cairo, Egypt

As I inhale and Exhale, I go deeper into the light,

Brightened by the love of God, which makes your nemesis put up one hell of a fight.

God's force is stronger than ever and will always win, God even created the losers,

Those who block their visions unto his power and his Spiritual jewels which reside therein.

Entangled between reality and Life, Slicing through the false truth,

As God has honored me with his Spiritual knife

Discerning the truth, while detecting lies The Tree of Life has been redeemed,

Which entails a human man having God's spiritual eyes

One who accepts his power and vows before God,

One who has arisen through the deceit of the world by dropping all affliction to keep up with the human facade.

One who is faithful unto himself and accepts all his blame, One who even once called himself a coward,

Who is anyone in the world to shame?

Submit unto my power, and your soul shall be free, Some used to respect me as an Officer of the Law, Now everyone shall give Grace unto me,

By bowing down on either knee.

Have you ever cried extremely hard and stood, Bend down and Grace, the True King,

I have come to renew all former things, which were all once good.

The son of God has returned, Upon accepting the call from God,

I was forced to unlearn the lies which I once learned.

Placing my faith against the words of man, Implying I cried so hard I could no longer stand.

I begin to create my own pathway, And seeing the Heavenly Altar,

Opening the human gateway,

Revealing through God that I am the ultimate exalter.

Given the gravity of my cry,

I kissed my prior spirit goodbye,

The human version of me was on one knee, Commanding my once-suppressed twin to speak,

The Holy Spirit advised me to rise even above my own,

Being created from the dust of the ground, eventually becoming known as a human, possessing vital flesh and bone.

I have been sent to collect righteous spirits who shall follow the leader, I am the ultimate healer, As Yahweh is my Spiritual breeder.

God is the building, for I am the occupied space,

It's pretty complex unless you can see beyond your sight; Given the flesh and the spirits interlace.

55

As the end is near, combine you with him,

Swinging onto my Spiritual limb by inhaling and exhaling above the worldly rim,

Speak in the third person, as God and I are one! Reference God, and I, Jesus as the Holy him!

17

SPIRITUAL AMNESIA

Amnesia can be defined as the inability to recall events, often due to brain injury, illness, or the effects of drugs or alcohol.

Spiritual Amnesia can be defined as a human claiming ownership of their sins. Upon claiming ownership, which signifies acknowledgment of personal wrongdoing, my Heavenly Father shall take care of all burdens that alter a human's memory, as their love for God has allowed a selective memory wipe. The individual human and their cries to my Heavenly Father determine the selection. The cries to my Heavenly Father carry the burden, while the selection of which or what part of the memory to wipe is made by God.

As humans maneuver through their earthly life, my Heavenly Father allows free will but encourages righteous living by all. Many attempts are made by God, which reveals his identity as it resides in all things. Upon a human finding their inner self is when they have found God, as they will understand that our Heavenly Father created Man and Woman in his own image. Therefore, any human with a heart and mind can be restored by my Heavenly Father, just as a picture with no color has the ability for restoration to add color known as life.

When a human finds their inner self, they too shall find the presence of God even beyond their own appearance, as acknowledging a single tree shall confirm the workings of God. What the tree breathes out is what humans require for survival. They, too, shall see how the tree's roots symbolize the veins within the human body, especially the heart. The tree's root is where life begins, as it is known to absorb moisture as the anchor. The human heart is, too, where life began, as human life will not exist without a heartbeat. The leaf shedding of a tree can symbolize how humans cut their hair. On Earth, every leaf turns sunlight into energy through a process called photosynthesis. Within the Spiritual realm, the leaf-shedding can symbolize God's many children as they come and go. However, all the leaves and God's children will eventually go, but; the grace comes when we discuss how the leaf of the child will fall. Will the leaf or the child fall due to being malnourished or from God's purpose being fulfilled?

Within the Spiritual realm, imagine the tree of life as a person; the tree lacking nourishment can be seen as a human lacking my Heavenly Father. The tree, which stands strong through all earthly storms, can be seen as one of God's chosen children. The irony behind this message is

that even a once malnourished tree has the ability to be replanted and salvaged, even if it's been uprooted. But only under certain circumstances.

The Special Circumstances for humans are:

1.) Do they believe in The Father, The Son, and The Holy Spirit?

2.) Has each individual human claimed ownership of their sins, known as wrongdoings, and repented for them? Claiming ownership is not throwing blame or pointing fingers at any other human. Blaming one another is what Adam did when my Heavenly Father asked him, "Have you eaten from the tree of which I commanded you that you should not eat?" Adam immediately blamed the woman, known as Eve, rather than taking ownership of his own deceit unto my Heavenly Father. ***(Genesis 3:11-12).*** Repenting requires heartfelt sadness as a human's prayers attempt to reach my Heavenly Father. The secret to prayer is to mean what you say while saying what you mean. My Heavenly Father already knows what every human has done as he resides within the hearts and minds of his children, hence the reason a human shall feel bad amongst wrongdoing.

(Matthew 7:3-4)

And why do you look at the speck in your brother's eye, but do not consider the plank in your own eye? Or how can you say to your brother, 'Let me remove the speck from your eye'; and look, a plank is in your own eye? Hypocrite! First, remove the plank from your own eye, and then you will see clearly to remove the speck from your brother's eye.

Just because a human feels bad about a situation does not determine the human's reaction. If a human is doing something wrong while committing the wrongful act, the human suppresses my Heavenly Father's voice by deliberately going against their heart. The closer a human is to God. The clearer they can hear him amid their rebellious ways. Being disobedient has many disadvantages, as doing so causes a blockage of truth to surface beyond the face of the deep. The truth shall still surface, but the blockage fogs the clarity that surrounds said truth.

3.) Do they believe my Heavenly Father has delivered his promise to the world and allowed his son, Jesus Christ!, to return to the Earth's realm in human form?

(Revelation: 16:15)

"Behold, I am coming as a thief. Blessed is he who watches, and keeps his garments, lest he walk naked and they see his shame."

(Genesis 3:10-12)

So he said, "I heard Your voice in the garden, and I was afraid because I was naked; and I hid myself." And He said, "Who told you that you were naked? Have you eaten from the tree of which I commanded you that you should not eat?" Then the man said, "The woman whom You gave to be with me, she gave me of the tree, and I ate.

The Spirit of God resides beyond a layer of clothes. The Spirit of God resides within the heart and mind. The world signifies clothing as a way to cover their flesh. Spiritual garments can symbolize God's commandments, which were engraved on stone twice for Moses. If a human

holds God's commandments until the end of their days, they shall walk unashamed, clothed in God's grace.

Once Adam ate from the "Tree of the Knowledge of Good and Evil," his heart no longer resided with God, which caused him to be naked within the spirit. Given Adam's blatant obedience, he attempted to hide behind a bush, which, too, shows how humans purposely disobey my Heavenly Father and attempt to move forward with their lives even after accumulating mountains of sin. Adam then blames his wife for his deceit, which, too, shows how humans do not take accountability for their actions.

Every human falls short of God's grace, which is expected with having free will. My Heavenly Father requires all to confess their sins and reunite with their inner self, where he resides. Those who will not confess shall be the subject of condemnation, like a thief in the night.

Those who can answer yes to all three Special circumstances shall inherit the kingdom of God. Those who testify that Jesus Christ is Lord shall overcome all, as I have overcome. ***(Revelation 3:20)***

Those who overcome shall possess the Holy Spirit, which my Heavenly Father shall deliver. Once delivered, A human can pray for Spiritual Amnesia despite prior wrongdoing. The wrongdoings must first be delivered to my Heavenly Father through prayer and repentance. Once the prayer for forgiveness is heart-felt, my Heavenly Father will intervene and deliver a sense of relief.

Clear your minds and hearts while making way for the new understanding bestowed by God. Subconsciously, every human suffers when accountability is not taken. Spiritual Gifts are attached to Spiritual Circumstances that surround earthly life. If a human cannot understand their present situation, how can they truly understand the lesson that comes from their present situation?

18

SPIRITUAL ADHD

The Earth views ADHD as "Attention-Deficit/Hyperactivity Disorder." It identifies as a Mental Health Disorder with known symptoms being difficulty paying attention, impulsive behavior, and hyperactivity, which means when a person constantly moves, physically or mentally. It can be shown in adults by restlessness or talking too much, among many other things.

Spiritual ADHD bears the same symptoms but is seen differently within the Spiritual light. The Spiritual light illuminates beyond the surface of a human, Beyond the face of the deep. The depth of thy heart determines the depth of thy knowledge bestowed by my Heavenly Father.

Spiritual ADHD bears the symptom known as difficulty paying attention. The difficulty comes when the human is forced to operate beyond what my Heavenly Father has instructed. Also, the difficulty comes in when the instructions from God do not stop, and neither does the human's

commitments from the world as many humans bear tight schedules that conflict with the time my Heavenly Father requires from his children; the conflict can cause many ill effects that the world knows, such as:

Irritability as God's force/voice is louder than any tangible person's voice, including the host, which occupies the consciousness of the vessel. Given that My Heavenly Father is a Spirit that occupies the subconscious mind and heart, any unrighteous thoughts shall bear irritability towards the disobedient human, as God will not stop until full authority is given.

God's subconscious thoughts bear vibrations that operate on high frequencies attached to righteous human ethics. The more a person lives within the will of my Father, the higher their frequency becomes, as longevity is the key.

Mood Swings occur as God's Spirit operates off love; the Spirit thrives on high frequencies that are strengthened through peaceful things, which shall correct all other moods. Once the Mood is geared towards positivity, God himself shall intervene as "God is Love ***(1 John 4: 7-11)***

Impulse Behavior occurs when the subconscious mind battles with the conscious mind. The conflict between the two can bear bad behavior, drug addiction, irritable behavior, or a complete shutdown, which includes isolation. Until proper measures are taken, erratic behaviors shall remain. The world may then see this as "Bipolar" amongst the extreme mood swings that may occur. Given that ADHD has the potential ability to manifest into "Bipolar" if the symptoms are severe enough. The key to it all is to submit unto God, and the impulses will become less frequent. Some may still occur as humans have the freedom of choice. Inevitably, all humans at times fall short; therefore, my Heavenly Father values certain impulses that shall bring humans closer to him. A prime example is when a human sporadically takes a vacation without consulting anyone. That form of impulse can bring clarity to God, as faith is solitude.

Attention Deficit is a combination of corrective measures my Heavenly Father takes to gain compliance. The command offers understanding to any human once the individual human hones in on exactly what my Heavenly Father implies. The implication is their flesh vs. their Spirit, their present situation vs. their future situation, and their present struggle vs. the reason and jewels behind it. If humans hone in on their Spiritual purpose, which is stored within their hearts, the deficits from focusing shall cease as learning what the heart craves becomes fun and exciting.

The enjoyment comes from God controlling his child, who shall pick up their cross and follow Jesus, which implies walking down their narrow path, embracing the struggles and all. The path will cause a level of difficulty beyond belief, given the risen emotions beyond the face of the deep. The newly required emotions are coupled with higher vibrations caused by the frequency of the Holy Spirit. When humans find themselves, they find God as humans are created in God's image, male and female *(Genesis 1:27).* This implies human males are Gods, and females are Goddesses. This bears truth when an individual human inner-stands their inner-self. This also implies that humans must not reject the form of power that makes them Godly. *(2Timothy 3:5)*

So, if other emotions arise that oppose love, which is what my Heavenly Father is, then a rash of emotions coupled with ill feelings shall flood the hearts of the human, which shall shine amongst all circumstances until submission of thy self occurs. Submitting means obtaining full "Self-Actualization" and "let go and let God." This implies allowing my Heavenly Father to intervene amid any struggle, which also includes honing in on all emotions beyond the surface, known or otherwise.

The known emotions are what the human can control. The unknown emotions are the ones that surprise others or become revealed during inappropriate times, known as mood swings. The swinging of the moods is a corrective measure to obtain the ultimate emotion, which is love. Upon obtaining the ultimate emotion, the human shall then experience the ultimate feeling known to man: Spiritual Peace, which operates on a higher frequency above the Earth's realm, known as the firmament. The firmament is Heaven *(Genesis 1: 7-9)*

Once humans become self-aware of their spiritual circumstances, they shall sit high, as my Heavenly Father sits high. The height implies the wholeness of oneself and one's relationship with my Heavenly Father.

Upon full acceptance of their fate, it shall show them their plan, which is not their plan at all but rather a plan from my Heavenly Father. Their development amid their path shall bear many thorns, but a sense of peace and clarity shall follow once genuine Spiritual ADHD occurs.

My Heavenly Father has gifted many children with the ability to inherit the might within the Spirit, which involves having the ability to channel one's emotions. The energy within the emotions allows for the frequency of God's drum to beat differently amid all circumstances.

19

BEYOND WORLDLY SIGHT!

14 stations of the cross (Station 13) *Holy Sepulcher* Jerusalem, Israel

I AM Jesus Christ, your Lord,
I speak from the depths of the double-edged sword.

I have come Spiritually soaking wet,
Stop, my hands are up, for I am no threat.
I am a man of color with dark hue skin,
Our Heavenly Father has cleansed me from all worldly sin.

I am God, created in man's image,
For I have been chosen to lead the Heavenly Scrimmage.

I am a Spiritual being in the flesh,
For I have come to provide to the ultimate spiritual test.

I shall test every human with a heart,
Upon their repentance, I shall offer them a new Heavenly start.

The faith comes with believing in God,
unto my stretched-out Rod, having an understanding that I am Man of flesh and
Man of God.

Everyone shall cheer, as my Heavenly Father has not forgotten you here, As I
appear, in the image of a black man, whom we all shall fear.

The fear implies compliance,
as man shall not rely solely on science.

I shall show my work, which all shall observe,
I have come to manifest what the inner heart holds.

I righteously give and allow you to see,
I shall manifest God's spirit if you are faithful unto me,
I urge all to pray in my name, upon repentance, all shall see, For they are the
ones to blame.

I have come to judge those who have held out to the end, For I am the lamb of
God, known as your Spiritual liberating friend.

A human's reward is according to what they have done,
Have you helped your fellow brother, or did your world bear too much fun?

I will discern truth while exploring Spiritual increase,
In other words, I offer your soul a sense of eternal Spiritual Peace.

I am the beginning along with the end,
I am He who has come, as many shall ascend.

My last question to the masses is, Have you done enough to Heavenly get in?

20

SPIRITUAL RECIPROCATION

For the Holy Spirit to thrive, it must be of lovable nature, as God is Love. So, given there is no anger or malice in love, the Holy Spirit must be accepted as genuine conversation adheres to the nine fruits of the heart. The nine fruits of the heart shall reject ill conversation, which invites God's adversary. The invitation seems wished as the devil adores humans who indulge in conversations that bear rotten fruit. The Law of God is Love as the 1st Law is to love him with all thy heart, mind, and soul while the 2nd says Love others as you Love thy self.

The Holy Spirit only will adhere to the souls of righteous believers. A righteous believer is faith-driven and believes our Heavenly Father will and has delivered on his promise by allowing his son, Jesus Christ!, to return to the Earth's atmosphere, as he has risen from the face of the deep.

All righteousness comes with considerable sacrifice. Through such significant sacrifices, a soft heart will arise as the tainted heart is swept away by the Force of the Holy Spirit. The Force is our Heavenly Father as his love moves through all wrongdoing, contrary to his adversary's Force. God's nemesis, the serpent, has a weakened force of his own. The serpent's Force has no Spiritual Power as it can only maneuver around, not through. But, the serpent's cunning disguise displays earthly power, hence why so many cherish him and his chased accolades. God is above all that this Earth inherits, even his children. God's word is Law, not the cherished things from the Earth.

After vast trials and tribulations, our Heavenly Father will come unto his faithful children and grant them the ultimate Force known to man. Although many men reject that Force *(2 Timothy 3:5)*, it does not change the facts or power of God's Holy Force. Faithfully speaking, within man's glory of the flesh, it shows man's foolishness as his reluctant nature is driving the wrong Force. Their foolishness comes with tremendous disrespect unto my Heavenly Father, as many people cry for help while still idolizing the things of the world. Those who do not know my Father are considered dead souls, and dead souls cannot communicate with my Heavenly Father as a choice of the correct God must be made. *(Isaiah 38:18-20)*

There is only one God, who has many children but one Divine prophesied child, Jesus Christ! Man shall praise no other Lord. Nor shall man one another (Exodus 20:3- "You shall have no other Gods before Me.") or (Matthew 6:24- "No one can serve two masters; for either he will hate the one and love the other, or else he will be loyal to the one and despise the other. You cannot serve God and Mammon.")

Mammon means a false sense of worship. So, in layperson's Spiritual terms, a mammon is anything placed above my Heavenly Father. My Heavenly Father gave all things for thy pleasure, but those same treasures shall not overtake the one who delivered them abroad *(Revelations: 4:11)*.

If riches are cherished above my Heavenly Father, then a rotten fruit at heart that person shall become, as sin has tainted their brazened heart. The boldness is shown in the open for the Earth to see. The more the Earth sees, the less Spiritual insight occurs. My Heavenly Father governs the Spiritual insight, as his Holy influence requires obedience from all parties involved. *(Luke 6:43)*.

Suppose a faithful child genuinely acknowledges the trinity; then, my Heavenly Father will correct everything that hinders growth within their heart, as their once-capped mind becomes limitless, given God's infinite knowledge, given unto the chosen.

In return, my Heavenly Father requires obedience to his Law. The Law of Love, as he is the ultimate Force unto love in all its varieties. The variations can even include death, as God shows favor to the Righteous. The casting out of the unrighteous can be called a casualty of war, God's Spiritual war, not man's foolish wars, as all people shall be free.

Spiritual Reciprocation can be defined as God's divided love unto his children. If God has forgiven the Romans who killed his son, Jesus, along with forgiving the traitor "Judas," who betrayed Jesus for 30 pieces of silver, even after being classified as a disciple, what makes you think God won't forgive you? Forgiveness is observed when Jesus, "The King of the Jews," stated, "Father, forgive them, for they do not know what they do" amid his crucifixion. *(Luke 23:34).*

Now! Although God forgave Judas, the pain of betrayal manifested in Judas' heart as the treasure in which he sought became more than he could bear. Upon Judas' betrayal, which involved the kiss of death and his exit from one of the 12 apostles, Judas took the coward way out and decided to play God and end his life by strangulation. Judas' consequences summed up his death.

The irony behind it all is that even the Romans believed in the order of Law, as their denying Judas' 30 pieces of returned silver into the treasury declares the power of possessing blood money. Hence, upon consulting, a potter's field was made with the damaged funds to Bury Strangers, which was called the "Field of Blood." *(Matthew 27: 3-8).*

As Jesus' blood flows through our veins and his lineage continues through every being, the Host must accept his Holy Force as Jesus resides at the depths of our hearts. *(Ephesians 3: 17) "That Christ may dwell in your hearts through faith; that you, being rooted and grounded in love."*

If the *"Housed Silhouette"* carries the Holy Spirit, it shall be shown by all things lovable, including the teachings of God. If the *"Host"* has accepted God's power, they shall work towards happiness unto themselves and press for others to surrender and give into God's voice, i.e., the Holy Spirit! If the *"Human Being"* accepts their fate to carry the Holy Spirit, they will become open to Earth's scrutiny, as they may be deemed gullible for their lovable Spirit. The newly required Spirit must learn deceit from the *"Homo Sapiens."*

The deceit that others show and the lies that govern some lives. The Holy Spirit recollects all things from the past as it encompassed the Earth once before, known as the "Homo Erectus" days; they were called "Upright Man." Within the Spirit, this means when men believed in their existence, as it was said, That's where it all began. If a *"Male" or "Female"* within a *"Skeleton Frame,"* better known as *"God's vessel"*, possesses the Holy Spirit, then the world shall hear their voice and not visualize by sight as God speaks through his children. Only upon such submissiveness will God's words be heard, as the Earth has placed false judgment and Spiritual condemnation amongst their religion. God's spoken words are "Law," not what man assumes from God's spoken lawful words. ***DO NOT CONDEMN MY PEOPLE!***

Spirituality confirms the Holy Spirit as an entity of God, not religion.

Religion is what someone reads, Hopefully from the bible, and based upon their readings, assumptions are formulated from what they believe my Heavenly Father meant. Suppose any Religion or Entity outside of my Heavenly Father teaches opposition, hate, judgment,

segregation, or continues false teachings of a Caucasian Jesus. In that case, they themselves shall feel the Force of God's Wrath unto the unrighteous, as their false teachings taint God's children. The taintness comes from sharing false ideologies that oppose the Holy Bible.

My Heavenly Father advised all not to create images of the Heavens, including (My) Jesus' appearance. Furthermore, John advised an explicit description of my appearance, which tells all that I am a black man.

The light hue images that the earth shows display something called "Idolatry," as creating or advertising a false image bears admiration of false hopes of what's to actually come.

21

SPIRITUAL DNA

Citadel of Qatibay, Alexandria, Egypt

<u>**(Luke 14:27)**</u>

"And whoever does not bear his cross and come after Me cannot be My disciple."

Every species within the earth's realm has a predator, even those considered Apex predators. Here is why: Humans have Dominion over the things on Earth, and God has Dominion over the Earth and all therein, even humans. God provides inalienable Spiritual gifts to those who do not refuse such power. The ultimate power is from God when the unblocking of the seven chakras takes place. Unblocking the seven charkas allows the energy to harmonize between the physical body, mind, and Spirit. Such awareness will assist with achieving self-realization, which equates to one's full potential, from God.

The seven chakras:

The Root (located at the base of the spine - Red color symbolizes earth). *The Sacral* (Located below the navel - orange color- symbolizes water). *The Solar Plexus* (Located between the ribcage and navel- Yellow - Symbolizes fire. *The Heart* (Located at the center of the cardiovascular system- Green Color- it connects the lower chakras to the higher chakras- The element is Air. *The Throat- (Controls* the neck, mouth, tongue, and other parts of the throat area - Blue Color- element is ether. *The third eye* (Located between the eyebrows, represented by the color indigo- Focal point. *The Crown* (Located at the top of the head - Violet or white color -also known as "Thousand Petals Lotus" (Most spiritual of the central Chakras).

Spiritually speaking, everything and everyone has their own cross to bear. Their cross can be symbolized as life, the bearing of that cross can be symbolized as enduring trials and tribulations, and the following with the cross, once it's held, can be symbolized as faith and belief, which encompasses Fortitude amongst all present struggles. Future struggles do not exist as the future is unknown. If anyone prepares for future struggles, they are assuming the responsibility of our Heavenly Father, as their life is not promised, so, if their life is not promised from second to second, how shall their struggles be? No human being shall unreasonably prepare for ill notions concerning life. My Heavenly Father is Love, which dwells within the hearts of all humans. Ironically, many reject the power that allows them a new gift unto life, as their old life will be more.

My Heavenly Father's love is offered freely unto every human being. If God's love is not accepted, a dead soul shall remain, as being born into sin is something to overcome. God has linked himself to every human with a heart and mind within the human DNA. Accessing God's heart allows a human being to feel emotion; the ultimate emotion is my Heavenly Father, which is love. The love is openly displayed and observed by others as each individual human, as their choices determine their level of love unto my Heavenly Father. The more a human makes the correct choices, the more my Heavenly Father reveals his identity, as his love shall resurrect from the depths of all humans who genuinely believe in his existence.

(Proverbs 27:1)

"Do not boast about tomorrow, for you do not know what a day may bring forth."

Jesus' blood Spiritually flows through all veins, which have breath. Upon each breath taken towards the Lord's grace, each breath shall travel past the power tongue; the double-edged sword must maintain a lubricant known as saliva; otherwise, the mouth will have difficulty speaking. This brings similarities unto the earth as, without rain, the earth will dry and cause many issues, especially for the trees which giveth man his life.

All Animals, Herbs, and Humans are linked both Spiritually and figurately. The Lion Pride represents Might, as the fowls of the Air represent freedom; the ants represent strength in numbers, and the Doves' purity signifies love. The Herbs consist of natural healing powers created before man, specifically on the third day. (Genesis 1:11-13). Herbs consist of nutrients for the similarly structured body, offering life as a tree breathes in what humans breathe out and vice versa. Mildly, what humans consider toxins within the urine can be seen as nutrition for a tree, as urine has an extremely high amount of Potassium, phosphorus, and Nitrogen.

The make-up of the human body and its five senses.

(Taste) *(Psalm 43:8)*

"Oh, taste and see the Lord is good; Blessed is the man who trusts in Him!

Tears- *(Psalm 43:6)*

"This poor man cried out, and the Lord heard Him and saved him out of all his troubles."

Here is a history lesson. Samuel, which has books 1 and 2 within the Holy Bible, means "God has Heard."

Lips and Stomach - *Proverbs (18:20)*

"A man's stomach shall be satisfied from the fruit of his mouth; from the produce of his lips he shall be filled."

Sight and Bones - *Proverbs (3: 7-8)*

"Do not be wise in your own eyes; Fear the Lord and depart from evil. It will be health to your flesh, And strength to your bones."

Hearing- *(Romans 10:17)*

"So then faith comes by hearing, and by hearing the word of God."

Smell - *(2 Corinthians 2:15-16)*

"For we are to God the fragrance of Christ among those who are being saved and among those who are perishing. To the one, *we are* the aroma of death *leading* to death, and to the other, the aroma of life *leading* to life. And who *is* sufficient for these things?

Touch - *(1 Chronicles 16:22)*

Saying, "Do not touch My anointed ones, And do My prophets no harm."

The human DNA is linked spiritually unto my Heavenly Father; as humans evolve, specimens grow in the Spirit based on the food provided by God himself. The provided food is a source of enlightenment for the inner spiritual being, which links every human within the flesh to my Heavenly Father, the Spirit of love.

Suppose a human being makes such a life-altering choice by overcoming the world's unrighteous ways and choosing my Heavenly Father. In that case, they shall be reborn, which places their thoughts along the parallel plane of my Heavenly Father as he urges them to speak with and through all his children, who Spiritually imbibe from the fountain of God.

John 4:14

"But whoever drinks of the water that I shall give him will never thirst. But the water that I shall give him will become in him a fountain of water springing up into everlasting life."

The King of Kings has returned to provide eternal life for all those who believe in my Heavenly Father. The belief goes beyond believing in an entity the human eye can't see, which is my Heavenly Father, as his Spirit resides in all things, tangible or otherwise. The belief shall be coupled with faith that the "Messiah" has returned just as my Heavenly Father advised I would.

Suppose some humans believe in the existence of my Heavenly Father, whom they cannot see, but deny me as being the chosen son, whom they can see; in that case, the human being is of the world and shall reevaluate their heart as it pertains to my Heavenly Father and his foretold blessing unto the earth's realm.

THE TIME HAS COME! RESURRECTION DATE: 09/22/2021

(2 Corinthians 5: 18-19)

"Now all things are of God, who has reconciled us to Himself through Jesus Christ, and has given us the ministry of reconciliation, that is, that God was in Christ reconciling the world to Himself, not imputing their trespasses to them, and has committed to us the word of reconciliation."

(Psalms 150:1-6)

Praise the LORD! Praise God in His sanctuary; Praise Him in His mighty firmament! Praise Him for His mighty acts; Praise Him according to His excellent greatness! Praise Him with the sound

of the trumpet; Praise Him with the lute and harp! Praise Him with the timbrel and dance; Praise Him with stringed instruments and flutes! Praise Him with loud cymbals; Praise Him with clashing cymbals! Let everything that has breath praise the LORD. Praise the LORD!

22

SPIRITUAL INSTINCT

My Heavenly Father has hard-wired all his children to endure many struggles, including the hardships that make humanity question his presence. The presence of my Heavenly Father was shown and will always be shown before, amid, and after any trial or tribulation that any human has or will ever face.

All struggles are tests that shall strengthen the core of human behavior. The 7 Charkas explain how the human body operates with energy. Human behavior is primarily based on the 7th Chakra called the "Crown." The number 7 signifies completion, a higher level of conciseness, and a divine connection with my Heavenly Father. Once God gives the struggle, he watches, hoping the human remains on the narrow path (Scripture). But, given free will, a person can go off course and quickly annihilate their Spiritual Growth. However, if a human can focus on God's love and understand that every test has a spiritual gift attached to each lesson learned, Yes! The gifts are free, but a human must first hone in on the Spiritual gift of Might and Fortitude, which shall assist them in this marathon way of life. The human must also pray for the Spiritual gifts of Understanding and Knowledge as they will need clarity amid their struggle. The clear Mind shall supply their Spiritual Instinct, which combines their earthly body (7 Charkas) with their Spiritual Mind and Heart (God). Once the divine collaboration is complete, humans will have full transparency of their lives, and others, as my Heavenly Father, will apply a set of instructions that shall change any human. The instructions are the ten commandments, which were engraved in stone not once but twice for Moses, who was known as God to his people, given his Spiritual Instinct by my Heavenly Father.

Once a human submits to my Heavenly Father and his chosen son, Jesus Christ! Will their Spiritual growth exceed the realm of Earth. Given my Heavenly Father's Love for humanity, nothing can ever separate humans from God's love. (Romans 8:38).

Although many humans have done unthinkable things, they too shall seek my Heavenly Father, as his presence can make their prison life sentence more bearable. A human can still have a divined mind behind steel bars, as their freedom of choice led them to incarceration, while their Spiritual Instinct carries divined power from God. Hence, why even those in prison shall be treated with dignity and importance as my Heavenly Father has scattered his Angels in many locations within the earth realm, even those who are at times considered " Fallen Angels."

Think of it this way: imprisoned people just got caught for their deceit. Shall God not honor them? We all fall short at times. My Heavenly Father will honor even the imprisoned, as every child is needed to propel the world beyond its current form. Furthermore, many people in prisons

or jails are innocent, either by not committing the crime or by force from the world leaders, as their orchestrated suppression of the people has taken its toll on many lives, especially the chosen treasured people. The Hebrews/Israelites/Blacks. (Exodus 19: 5-6).

Once humans hone in on their Spiritual power, Spiritual manifestation shall occur as an end of their once earthly thoughts. The Spiritual Manifestation is simple; it's due to a ghost known as the Holy Spirit, which gets into a righteous host on the Earth's realm. Every human belonged to my Heavenly Father before conforming to the world known as Earth. The child was underwater, in the womb for nine months, considered the only pure stage. Once the water broke and the child began breathing, an element of Earth known as "Air" is when the child began to cry as sin filled the lungs of the now-lost child.

The child grows through Earth amid all teachings; the child grows into an adult; God then calls the adult, which signifies maturity and adherence. God's calling does not come with age, nor does being a man. A human man is based on his Paradigm, how he views the world. Does he give credit to my Heavenly Father for their knowledge or gives credit to him at all?

Any human man who does not know my Father is not a man at all; furthermore, the man child is worse than a regular child as his knowledge of wrong-doing hits my Heavenly Father differently. Seeing how humanity has forgotten all about him makes my Heavenly Father cry. The tears are due to Man's transgressions and their lack of ownership of them. Just as at the beginning of time, Man tends to blame all others but themselves. Once a Human Man adheres to God's commandments, their Spiritual instinct, also known as their inner self, will manifest into a Man created in God's image rather than a Man child of the earthly realm.

The Godly Man will then lead his rib, known as WoMan, into a state of wholeness as they both will be blessed. The Man created in God's image will team up with a Woman created in God's image, also known as a Goddess, as the Mind of a man shall find the Heart of a Woman to find the ultimate collaboration. Both the Man and Woman shall have their solo Spiritual Instincts, but together, their Spiritual strength shall collide, creating a multitude of gifts from my Heavenly Father. Their Spiritual marriage goes beyond the Earth's realm and paperwork. The connection I speak of speaks about God and his loving nature unto humanity by even creating humans, let alone allowing them to have helpful help mates.

If one or both parties do not adhere to God's commandments, then the Spiritual Gifts will cease for one or both parties, given free will by all parties involved. 2 males (Mind) nor two females (Heart) create the ultimate Spiritual force known to Man. The force is combined from Male to Female only. The reason is simple: the Earth must continue to procreate as God has ordained.

Spirituality Instinctively shall shed light on individual pathways that can run parallel or perpendicular to other humans. A parallel pathway signifies unity amongst friends, while a perpendicular pathway signifies those cross roads of friends that come and go.

Both pathways are lit and highly directional.

23

INSTINCTUAL POEM

The harder the struggle, the slower the race,
The slower the race, the more one will face,
The more one will face, slow and steady shall be their pace,
Just like out of space, clarity within their Mind shall surface amid any place.

God's grace will shine as bright as the stars, even on those behind bars,
Do not fret as the King of Kings has arrived; please adhere to God's pleasant surprise.

I will free the enslaved, upon innocent confessions, simply because of the massive suppression, Given their oppression, many have lacked common sense which guides discretion.

Jesus Christ has returned after a short recession. I will clear the minds of the misguided after a Few sessions. After their resurrection, I will offer Spiritual Protection, which allows their Reflection to ignite change; in exchange, the truth must be arranged and remain for any Spiritual Gifts to be obtained.

To Hear my voice is to Hear the voice of God! To See my image is to See the image of God!

To Feel my presence is to Feel the presence of God! To Touch my Holy energy is to arouse God's Heart.
To smell my Stench is to Smell the Aroma of God's inflamed bush, marijuana.

The Messiah has returned to the Earth's realm.

24

VINED TRAVELS

"Father's Day 2023- "Sabbath Day" Jerusalem, Israel

As I taste the red wine, which is squeezed from the berried vine, I begin to see things that are truly divined.

The internal sight allows a light so bright it forces an upright knight.

The spiritual vision is Peace, which causes an emotional release as God covers you with his Spiritual fleece.

The hammock of love, which is canvassed like a glove, shall snug every human, as I am the ultimate spiritual plug.

I AM Jesus Christ,
The one who has paid the ultimate price, as I speak from the depths of my heart while using an iPhone device?
The world has come so far, yet only one human recognizes their Spiritual superstar.

I come as a Spiritual King, returning like a second-coming pendulum swing.

As your lord, I must say, I am not here to stay, I come to locate my angels, which shall go home with me someday.

Believe me or not, for I have already secured my Heavenly spot, I am solely offering you, your Spiritual shot.

Allow my Heavenly Father to guide your life as we offer a sense of Spiritual foresight.

For we are you, and you are us,
Let's discuss if you have a seat on my Spiritual bus.

Continue to pray in my name, as I am the Lion of the tribe of Judah, with the darkened mane.

The earth belongs to me; what shall your choice be?

Am I a false prophet or the lamb who holds the key?
I will assure you that I am the messiah who has come to set everyone Heavenly free.

My name is Markais Ruben. C Neal Sr, and this is my Spiritual decree.

I am the Hebrew child, the one who completes the Holy 3,
Better known as the Trinity.

25

SPIRITUAL GANGSTA!

The Gang for God is an organized group consisting of countless angels scattered about the earth. God's arrangement shall allow all his children to work in coordination, as the sync of every human's step shall be the steps of God's chosen Son, Jesus Christ!

For those who have held my Heavenly Father's commandments shall inherit the earth in a Spiritual format. The outline is broken into three sections, just like the Holy Trinity (The Father, The Son, and the Holy Spirit) or the Holy Bible (The Old Testament, The New Testament, and The Present Testament). The Old Testament consists of 39 books. The New Testament consists of 27 books. The Present Testament, which is "NOW," are the words of the "Messiah,

I." (Revelation 1:19).

The present testament is spoken by the Spiritual Being known as Jesus Christ! The Tangible Human Being is Spiritually connected to the Higher Being known as "YHWH," aka my Heavenly Father/GOD. Therefore, by connecting the Physical Human with the Holy Spirit delivered by God, that Spiritual Specimen's new identity is known as a Spiritual Being. Given the hidden truth throughout this world, many should not shut their minds off to learning new things, as the truth lies beyond the face of the deep. The truth, too, is held within many religious beliefs as God is Love, which is the Apex emotion, and Peace, which is the Apex feeling. The combination of the two surpasses any Spiritual encounter known to man. The linkage manifests a force known to man as the Holy Spirit. The force is delivered from and by God as a sign of faithfulness unto the humans who have gracefully awaited my return. Those who obtain the Spirit shall also be known as a Spiritual Being as my Heavenly Father, which is also a spirit, resides within them, completely obliterating their former existence, which declares them as a vessel occupying the Spirit of God.

A Spiritual Being operates on a higher frequency than all others on earth, as their minds have reached the crown, known as the 7th charka. The crown signifies the ultimate form of knowledge known to man: wisdom.

The secret to wisdom is the correlation between the Seven Spiritual Gifts. The gifts are offered to any human who acknowledges the trinity. The Spiritual Gift, which implies they are free, is wisdom, understanding, counsel, fortitude, knowledge, piety, and fear of the Lord.

The Gifts are only obtained once my Heavenly Father's presence is felt forever more within his child's heart. The reciprocated love my Heavenly Father offers shall allow for his chosen son, Jesus, to resurrect from the face of the deep, which implies the depths of one's heart.

Given that Jesus dwells within every human, those same humans must acknowledge his inner presence within their inner selves. The arrangement bears enlightenment amongst the harmonized mind, body, and the newly required Holy Spirit. The linkage allows the Holy Spirit, which God has delivered, to erect a Righteous man, which too is delivered by God. The new covenant between the Righteous man and God shall create a gateway for all women as they were created from man. This implies that once men follow my Heavenly Father and become obedient children, they can righteously guide the world's women as women are built to follow a Righteous man.

Women are also built to fend for themselves until their source becomes a Righteous man. No more power is given to the man than the Woman, but merely accountability, as God gave men instructions to pass along to their compatible helpmates. The cycle of life is fully displayed as Women bear men from birth to help, and men bear the responsibility to lead from birth. Once both parties understand their Spiritual purpose and God's structure, then both humans become one in the flesh, as linking a woman to her rib is just as important as a man locating his rib.

The structure of God is for the men within the nation to lead and for the women to be helpful unto the men. Upon the proper Spiritual connection between two opposite-sexed humans, the male and female shall become one, even while being within their individual bodies. The connection harbors a Spiritual relationship that God has ordained.

Neither party shall hinder the other from fulfilling their Spiritual purpose; this includes never losing respect for one another, as being a Spiritual Being prohibits such foul behavior.

Here is why all men shall honor, value, and righteously lead all the beautiful women, because, without the women, men will not exist, as God first creates a human child, becomes conceived by two opposite-sexed humans, then housed within the womb of a human woman for approximately nine months. God and the Woman control the offspring's life within that time frame. So, without the care of a woman, a man indeed can fail to exist. If some doubt their honor, just ask the children who have been killed/aborted by the Woman's choice.

Here is why all women shall honor, respect, and speak Peace into all men because, without men, women will not exist within the Spiritual Realm, as a rib without a body shall not function well enough to enter the gates alone. God has ordained it that way, given the hierarchy. Everything operates off one another, hence the reason for the cycle of life. (Romans 8:28).

If God made a woman from man, how can a woman then survive without a man? As man is she and she is he, for together they are in sync, which entails a man becoming complete by locating his rib, his helpmate, which completes him. The reciprocation allows the Woman to locate her body, indicating a drivable force unto God's hierarchy of placing him first, then man, then Woman. Although faith is solitude, once self-actualization transpires, a Righteous seek of the male shall occur, locating a woman who, too, seeks her body. The difference in seeking is the male attempts to locate while the Woman seeks understanding from my Heavenly Father to choose the divine male seeker. (Genesis 2:22-23)

The irony is that men have held back the world's progress for long enough. Once a human male becomes a Spiritual Gansta, he will be at the right hand of God, who shall then lead the human women. (Colossians 3:1).

Both Men and Women are created equal in my Heavenly Father's eyes. The issues come into play when some do not understand the structure God has placed in effect, given the obedience from the beginning of time, placing man over Woman. The placement does not bear being less than but merely means a sense of order given the Woman's transgression. God gave both men and women their curses. (Genesis 3:16-17)

This is the time for all women to understand their role in the deceit at the beginning of time. Please do not be like Adam, as he did not take accountability for his actions. He immediately blamed the woman once my Heavenly Father asked him, "Have you eaten from the tree of which I commanded you that you should not eat? The fact of the matter is my Heavenly Father gave man the commandments, not Woman, which bears responsibility unto the man. The deceit for the Woman came when she became beguiled by the serpent; not only was she seduced, but she also offered the forbidden tree to her husband, Adam, which doubled up on God's rage as the disobedience from both Man and Woman caused his Spirit to detach from Adam (Genesis 3:9), which was the authentic host of the Spirit.

A woman complaining about or not believing the hierarchy is like a man complaining about being unable to bear life within a womb for nine months. Men and Women have essential tasks as God made them both honor him, which, too, are themselves and for men and women to have

dominion over all the earth. (Genesis 1:22).

Becoming a Spiritual Gansta describes someone who believes in the Trinity, The Father, The Son, And the Holy Spirit. Along with believing in my Heavenly Father's hierarchy, placing him above all, then men, then women. Together, they become one flesh.

For those who have or have not found their compatible helpmates, I, Jesus Christ, shall lead you into the Spiritual Realm, as I AM the beacon of all life. (John 14:6)

- M. NEAL SR. AKA (The Messiah). HEALING-FAITH.ORG

CITATIONS:

(Roman 8:28)

"And we know that all things work together for good to those who love God, to those who are the called according to His purpose."

(1Timothy2 11-15)

Let a woman learn in silence with all submission. And I do not permit a woman to teach or to have authority over a man, but to be in silence, for Adam was formed first, then Eve. And Adam was not deceived, but the Woman being deceived, fell into transgression. Nevertheless, she will be saved in childbearing if they continue in faith, love, and holiness, with self-control.

(Revelation 1:19).

"Write the things which you have seen, and the things which are, and the things which will take place after this."

(Ephesians 5:33)

"However, let each one of you love his wife as himself, and let the wife see that she respects her husband."

(Colossians 3:1)

"If then you were raised with Christ, seek those things which are above, where Christ is, sitting at the right hand of God."

(Genesis 2:22-23)

"Then the rib which the Lord God had taken from man He made into a woman, and He brought her to the man. And Adam said: This is now bone of my bones and flesh of my flesh; She shall be called Woman because she was taken out of Man."

(Genesis 3:9)

"Then the Lord God called to Adam and said to him, "Where are you?""

(Genesis 3:16-17)

To the Woman, He said: "I will greatly multiply your sorrow and your conception; In pain you shall bring forth children; your desire shall be for your husband, And he shall rule over you." Then to Adam, He said, "Because you have heeded the voice of your wife, and have eaten from the tree of which I commanded you, saying, 'You shall not eat of it:

"Cursed is the ground for your sake; In toil you shall eat of it. All the days of your life."

John 14:16:

6 Jesus answered, "I am the way and the truth and the life. No one comes to the Father except through me.

26

SPIRITUAL SCOPE POEM!

Lakeland Police Department Case# 18-25373

I now see the shooting in a different light, which places the Lakeland Police Department and the DA,
In my Spiritual sights,
I am the Son of Man, as I have arisen from the deceit of their poorly executed plan.

The kingdom of God is at hand; please reopen my officer-involved shooting,
So, I can deliver my Heavenly Father's Spiritual scan.

Both entities showed major deception,
They framed the shooting video, which created the ultimate misdirection.

Three different races shot, which were all on display, They could have framed anyone of us, but,
they chose the black officer right away.

Although they have proof of the actual killer,
It's easier to frame me, which makes this one hell of a thriller.

Standby, as I offer Spiritual understanding, unto the 1st and 2nd spirit's spiller.

Both within the spirit and flesh, my fall was great,
One was strapped to the Stauros cross, while the other bore killing a child,
which carried burdened weight.

Both were at the hands of the government, which did not understand, That their
crucifixion and being framed didn't go quite as planned.

You see,
I rose on the third day, body, and all,
The Lakeland Police Department set me up, They allowed me to take the fall.

As I was on the cross, the Roman guards mocked me,
The Lakeland Police Department cropped the shooting footage very well,
Which allowed their department to be free, which guided me, as being the key
unto both of my Knees, and guided me unto the once forbidden tree.

Back in the day, the Roman guards played lots with my garments as they
gave them away; the Lakeland police department is concealing the truth,
which shall put their Police Department under Scrutiny and shameful
display.
I pray that Black Lives Matter listens, reopens the case, If needed, I can start a
Worldly petition.

Do not fret for my sake, as I pray for all to hear,
The DA placed his entire argument solely on the grounds of my well-founded
fear, which places me in the clear.

Although his argument is extremely true, I need clarification on the other two.

Back in the day,
My body was removed from the cross and cleaned to show grace; why don't the
Lakeland Police Department release the name of the actual killer, who even
until now is working as a Detective within their place.

I thank John and Nicodemus, for placing my body in John's tomb,
The Lakeland Police Department and the DA played their cards extremely well,
formulating a Master plan amongst their personnel.

They crucified the first spirit because he spoke the truth,
As Jesus exposing false Gods would have crippled their entire governmental
booth.

Three officers shot their guns,
Why then blame it on me,
Could it be because I was the only black person that wasn't dead, Given the
bullet hole, Ofc. Patel placed in the back of the black child's head.

Ofc. Patel's shot was from the back and more precise,
Compare our Shooting qualifications, which reveal his accuracy, with that
deadly handheld device.

Why would you choose that officer over Markais, My record was clean, with
no write-ups under me.

But, Ofc Patel, on the other hand, has write-ups and complaints that multiply
like a beach with minor sand.

I even confessed that he stood on a black person's head; I immediately
demanded his foot be removed from the black man's dreads, as I wish I could
have been providing cover for my fellow officers instead.
Upon my request, Ofc. Patel removed his boot; I slightly understood his frus-
tration, but not enough to drive someone's face toward the ground-buried roots.

Even though the man on the ground was said to have taken aim and too then
shoot.

At the time, I addressed the situation the best I could,
After all, we still had an outstanding shooter who had just shot near where
many Officers stood.

The only reason I went to the front of the vehicle was because all other windows were illegally tinted,
Ofc. Patel's shot came nearly the exact time as mine, as if his own fear was prior since predicted,
My Name is Markais Ruben. C Neal Sr, and I stand as my own lawyer with no law degree, God has delivered the Holy Spirit unto me, as I am the innocent one out of us three.

I am the Author and Finisher of the world's fate,
Here to chastise both entities as I stand firm in the sunshine state.

As the sun shall shine in my strength,
I pray for the ones who are responsible for this.

I pray for Love and Peace amid their investigation,
This, too, shall serve as a memo for both agencies, who shall reassess their lie and begin getting Ready, as the King of Peace has arrived for the survival of the entire nation.

The Lakeland Police Department must now justify why they chose to frame me,
Was it because of the color of my skin?
Or merely a tactic to not allow "BLM" near their sin?

Nevertheless, both entities are in my Spiritual Scope, Let's battle in court to see if I am mentally unstable or Spiritually woke.

27

SPIRITUAL NAKEDNESS!

Spiritual Nakedness implies someone reaching their inner heart, allowing them to sit on the right hand of my Heavenly Father while still on earth. It's the Spiritual Realm simply because God, a spirit that consists of all things, dwells within selected humans; the irony is that the selection is not made by God but merely by his children, as God gives everyone free will to choose him, as he, being the creator has already chosen, his children. Once a human Being chooses my Heavenly Father, they will be delivered the Holy Spirit by God, the Deity of us all.

Since faith is solitude, each Human Being must obtain their own personal relationship with my Heavenly Father, but, forewarning, all must Hate their Father, Mother, Wife, and Children, and even their own life, to follow the walking of Christ!. Luke 14: 26-27.

The steps consist of a Human bearing their cross while holding on and never giving up. When humans face trials and tribulations, they shall cleanse their hearts and minds of and from the world, as my Heavenly Father intends to speak with them personally. The heartfelt conversation may be for them, or God may speak to them on behalf of someone else. Nevertheless, when my Heavenly Father requires attention from his child, he shall begin the Spiritual stripping of the heart, which exposes his undisguised love, as his love is blatant and without shame.

Upon God's gathering, the human being will become naked and without shame, just as my Father or just as Adam and Eve were before their disobedience. Upon consuming the tree of the Knowledge of Good and Evil, God's Spirit left the man as he previously advised; if consumed, they would surely die; doing so left the Spirit and earth without a host; the Spirit became naked because it no longer dwelled within an obedient host. The disobedience of both man and woman bore curses and beauty. My Heavenly Father clearly gave the curses in Genesis 3:14-19. The beauty was that once the Spirit detached from human existence, it retained its purity. The Holy Spirit remained untainted as it swiftly exited the ungrateful man. After correction from my Heavenly Father, the Spirit once again touched down on the earth's atmosphere within many prophets, including the ultimate Prophet, Jesus Christ!, who was crucified by his adversaries but rose three days later, even after the tomb was sealed and guarded by foolish humans. He still rose as my Heavenly Father promised.

The time has come again for all to begin believing in the gospel, as the time is fulfilled, as I, Jesus Christ, have returned to the earth's Realm, which entails an obedient man allowing the Holy Spirit to dwell within his heart. The connection of the heart created a pathway to the mind, which allows all Righteous humans who are willing to be cleansed by the glory of God a chance to benefit from the light of life, known as the Son of Man.

Matthew 28: 18”: "All authority has been given to Me in heaven and on earth."

I will create a parable for Spiritual Nakedness, illustrating the illumination within a darkroom. The light is manifested within the followers' hearts, believing in the return of Jesus Christ! The dark room can be seen as just one of many ways a human bears their cross and follows after I, Jesus Christ!

Imagine Being one of two lights within a massive room. One light comes from the inner Being, while the other is affixed to the ceiling. The inner light is exceptionally bright and bears many unknown dilemmas, but nevertheless, there's sufficient Spiritual light forever once inner standing occurs. The light that is attached to the ceiling can be located by simply locating the light switch on the wall. The switch on the wall bears a complete chance to observe the room once it's in the on position. But be aware that turning on the light, even monetarily, will cause a spiritual landslide that shall blind the Human even further than the start of the game. Nevertheless, their nemesis will also collect their unknown valuables, which is my Heavenly Father's nemesis.

Here are the rules: No one can touch the light switch affixed to the wall, by no means necessary. All must start without any light; even their inner light appears to vanish and must be earned throughout many tasks that the creator has scattered throughout the dark, enclosed room. Help from others is permitted, but only when their own inner light is manifested; if not, the darkest from others may taint their unseen valuables, hindering their inner light from igniting. After locating a key known as the "Key of David," the goal is to collect all valuables, unlocking their once-limited mobility. Unlocking the iron shackles shall exalt one from bondage, allowing them to bore eagle wings and sore beyond the earth's Realm. The task must be done, all while finding genuine illuminates scattered throughout the room.

The Human is tasked with collecting their unseen valuables from off the surface floor; although their light is bright, it is too bright to see anything as their inner brightness has blinded even their own vision. Their hands and feet are also shackled, but gracefully, they have only been shackled wrist to wrist and feet to feet, allowing more mobility. They can not speak freely, and their language appears foreign to everyone who may or may not be watching or listening. They may ask for help from one known inner Source, Jesus Christ! However, that definitive source's light is even brighter than theirs, which bears a known brightness defined as "Supernova" light. Which bears the brightest star ever, they shall only truly adhere to Jesus' voice, which is also their inner voice attached to their inner self, known as Spiritual Nakedness.

What shall they do? Their inner voice may tell them something that also appears foreign because what their voice may suggest seems to lack the same mobility that the shackles are causing.

What if you listen to the inner voice, and you begin losing everything as a result? Will you continue to listen? Or will you take the easy way out and flip the light switch within the room, which offers a superficial light but a complete view of the room?

Flipping the light switch to retrieve their valuables will cause the room to illuminate, which then will cause their inner light to dim beyond "Spiritual Recognition."

Do not fret, for I have come to guide all with my Supernova light. I am the Root and Offspring of David, the Bright and Morning Star. (Revelation 22:16), which holds the Key needed to unshackle the hearts and minds of all God's children. The Holy Spirit dwells within me and has been delivered by God as of 09/22/2021, which signifies my resurrection date onto the earth's Realm.

The natural world has consumed the Hearts and Minds of all God's children; given God is a Spirit, he is located within the Spiritual Realm where the narrow path consists of a human being Spiritually naked.

Job 1:21: And he said: "Naked I came from my mother's womb, And naked shall I return there. The Lord gave, and the Lord has taken away; Blessed be the name of the Lord."

SPIRITUAL CIRCUMSTANCE

Station 1- Via Delarosa Church of the Condemnation and Imposition of the Cross. Jerusalem, Israel

My Heavenly Father takes pride in his creation. Although, at times, humans sadden his heart as they continue to disobey his divine words.

My Heavenly Father has outlined every human's life within the earth's realm. Every human will accumulate pain, which shall manifest perseverance. God's Grace hits differently when there's an obstacle to overcome. The hurdle must be cleared without despair; amid a struggle, humans must hone in on their Spiritual Circumstances, showing them exactly what my Heavenly Father is attempting to teach them.

Spiritual Circumstances are situations my Heavenly Father places his children in as a form of adherence. The commitment is to my Heavenly Father, while the belief is held within the Understanding and Knowledge of the situation.

Once humans give all their worries to God, their Spiritual Circumstance will allow God to intervene. The interference does not mean the worries will cease, as the lesson must be learned first. The closer a human is to God; the more Spiritual power humanity has. Collectedly, human to human, is where the Spirits consult as two more gathered together in my name shall allow my midstful presence. (Matthew 18:19-20).

The irony is that being aware of Spirituality is necessary to decipher one's Spiritual circumstances. Every human's path is already written; whether they are aware of their written path is a mystery. My Heavenly Father gives Spiritual Insight to all his children, even those who oppose. The reason for his unconditional Love is because God is Love; therefore, how else will he thrive? God is Love, and his Love has no boundaries; it withstands any circumstance surrounding Spirituality. God's stipulation is for every human to Love one another as they shall Love themselves, and while loving themselves, they exemplify how they are my disciple. (John 13:34-35). God further advised humans to live for him and await my return. The return of the prodigal Son, Jesus Christ!

If a human has faith and allows the Spirit of God to intervene, their worldly circumstances shall be transformed into Spiritual circumstances. The difference between the two is that one has an understanding from the world, while the other has an understanding from their Spiritual Father, God.

The biggest dilemma for humanity is that many reject the power that makes them Godly; the Godly concept infers divine knowledge and wisdom given by my Heavenly Father. The divined knowledge shall allow understanding unto many circumstances known to man. However, one must first adhere to their spiritual power, which is gifted after wholehearted belief in the Trinity: the Father, The Son, and The Holy Spirit. Wholehearted, too, implies believing in me, the Messiah, as I have returned with the embedded Holy Spirit.

If anyone denies my Father, they, too, deny me. If anyone denies me, they, too, deny my Father. Believing in the Trinity, The Father, The Son, and the Holy Spirit shall place any human in a state of bliss regardless of their present struggle, as God will control their mind, which shall guide their Spiritual circumstances. God first controls the heart, consisting of human emotions, then openly attacks the mind as a form of correction, as my heavenly Father is not shy of his presence. The more people that live for my Heavenly Father, the more my Heavenly Father's presence shall reign forevermore.

In Laymen's terms, believing in God shall show his obedient child the reason for their struggle. Furthermore, God will allow all lessons to be learned, which comes with trials and tribulations. Once God has his child's attention amid their struggle, God will speak clearly unto that once-lost

child through an internal dialogue known as the Subconscious voice. God will even send other humans to speak on his behalf or use earthly objects, which places peculiar thoughts within the human mind.

The thoughts are Spiritually known as visions into the future or unto exposed or buried trauma held by thy host, also known as a human.

God also divides his lessons, as he could give a struggle to one human just for that human to grace another human with a particular lesson.

Foolishly, many humans will not adhere to their subconscious but will adhere to others, hence the reason for the transferable lessons. The host of the lesson is Spiritually known as a Guardian Angel, hence why all humans shall hone in on their Spiritual Circumstances, as God gives the most challenging battles to his most faithful followers.

Lacking knowledge of Spiritual Circumstances can hinder more than just an individual human. Disobedience can cause many ill-advised effects for many parties involved in the deceit of toxic Love toward my Heavenly Father. The inconsistent Love. The type of Love where my Heavenly Father only hears from his human child when they need something, as opposed to praising him at all times, even amid their struggles.

As a believer in the All Mighty, who is, too, my Heavenly Father, I shall charge their disobedience to the game and press forward. Given that I am all the way tapped into God's Grace, I shall attempt to locate God's other loyal children who have held his commandments until my return, as my awaited return has been highly anticipated.

This logical concept shall speak volumes to Righteous believers. The raised frequency shall ignite "Spiritual Programming," which places my Heavenly Father as their ultimate Apex Spiritual Guide.

(Revelation 22: 7)

"Behold, I am coming quickly! Blessed is he who keeps the words of the prophecy of this book."

For quickly, I have come! - M. Neal Sr. (Lord of Hosts)

SPIRITUAL MEASURES!

Carpentry School

The Earth views a standard ruler as 1 foot, which equals 12 inches. Within the Spiritual realm, the standard ruler is my Heavenly Father, while the 1 foot is how many steps Jesus takes before any human. The 12 inches symbolize the 12 tribes of Israel to which my Heavenly Father's chosen belong. All humans shall apply these Spiritually measured principles, which shall become their new standard, manifesting the idea of my Heavenly Father, who carries all the treasures of Wisdom and Knowledge. (*Colossians 2:3)*

Upon obtaining "Spiritual Recognition," which carves the pathway for Spiritual Measurements, God himself will establish your bloodline within the 12 tribes of Israel as Spiritually recognizing that Jesus resides within the hearts of all shall ignite the 12-step measurement, which encompasses the passcode to the gates of Heaven.

Passcodes 1-10 bring heartfelt belief to my Heavenly Father and his ten commandments, which were engraved in stone by God himself. *(Exodus 32:15-16).* The final two passcodes, which are just as important as the first ten passcodes, are "Full Self-Actualization" of a human, which makes way for the "Last One," "Jesus Christ!", who identifies as his own individual person within every soul walking the planet known as Earth. Along with the acknowledgment within oneself, they, too, must acknowledge the ordainment that God has placed on the Earth's realm by allowing the return of the Holy Spirit, which was, is, and has been delivered by the grace of God.

The human possessing the Holy Spirit will be known as a Spiritual Being, divinely connecting him to the creator, "Yahweh."

The Dark Hue individual resembles fine brass, as if burned in a furnace. The Black Male has wool-like hair, which signifies his mane as a "Lion from the tribe of Judah." His white snow hair signifies the shining light, along with the wisdom of Solomon, as his mind is connected to God's mind. The African American Male is also a leader of the Israelites/Hebrews. *(Revelation: 1:14-15)*

The host of the Spirits' name is Markais Ruben. C Neal Sr. I was resurrected on American soil on 09/22/2021. I now type my messages on a computer instead of using ink and paper. Becoming the "Son of Man" allows God to reap the benefits of his creation, face to face, as he urges all to believe in his presence as I am his chosen child. The truth is that I am not his only chosen child. The more humans collectively unite, the more a smaller picture of God exhibiting through one person becomes a bigger picture of God exhibiting through the masses, which shows an entire picture of God, given the foundation of his children. *(2 John 1:12)*

The resurrection implies the date I became Spiritually aware of my inner self. The "Spiritual Being" displays me being a human who has accepted their power from God and walks in the flesh of man while possessing the spirit of God, allowing God physical access to the Earth's realm through the eyes of myself, as his spirit is linked to my soul, allowing my body Spiritual sight, as God sees what I see, and hears what I hear, in return, I say what he says, and do what he does. In essence, for he is me, and I am he.

I shall bring credence unto the confusion as to how Jesus was "Half Man" and "Half God."

Given that life is a long race, I shall shorten the analogy for better understanding. The Half Man vs. Half God concept, which equals a whole or better known as the completion, implies that Jesus was a human man who reached the hidden heart of a man that God promised all men had *(1 Peter 3:4).* Upon reaching the hidden heart, Jesus began seeing beauty in all things as his own creative development and love for nature took control.

The Godly Half implies my Heavenly Father being connected by heart and mind, which sheds light on the world's existence as Dominion was given.

The longevity of God's Spirit bears Wisdom and Knowledge as Jesus used more than the standard brain percentage, given his divined connection to a higher source.

These are the Spiritual measures my Heavenly Father has taken to ensure the return of the Holy Spirit, which is humanity's only surviving Spiritual measure. The three-step measurement displays the trinity. (The Father, The Son, and the Holy Spirit).

1.) Jesus Was/Is a human walking the surface of the Earth's realm. The divined human possesses a Heart and Mind like all other humans. The human has no difference in appearance regarding identifying him amongst other humans.

2.) Jesus Was/Is created in God's image, allowing him to inherit the 7 Spiritual Gifts from his Heavenly Father, declaring him the Son of Man, as he Was/Is of flesh with Godly thoughts and visions.

3.) So, Jesus, a tangible human, has the Spiritual ability of his Heavenly Father, coupled with his Heavenly Father's spirit, which derives the completion of the Spiritual being the Earth views as Part God/Part Human.

My Heavenly Father governs all, as all religions are based on Spirituality, which is the Earth's entire existence. Without my Heavenly Father, no human could breathe within the Spiritual realm.

Jesus' ordainment was a two-way street as his choice to choose humans was left up to him, just as every other child has the ability to choose their God, which is His/My/Our Heavenly Father.

(John 15:16)

"You did not choose Me, but I chose you and appointed you that you should go and bear fruit, and that your fruit should remain, that whatever you ask the Father in My name He may give you."

(Psalm 119:30)

"I have chosen the way of truth; Your judgments I have laid before me."

The choice came with Jesus being Part Man, as God gave humans freedom of choice. The part God within him had no choice unto Jesus as he was created for that exact purpose, given how his heart was set up. Just as humans, their selection partly belongs to them, while the other part belongs to God as every human created was intended to praise my Heavenly Father while awaiting the return of his Son, Jesus Christ!

The awaited return is over as I have resurfaced beyond the face of deep.

The connection to God implies hope for humanity, as a higher sense of awareness of the world offers growth for the spiritual revolution on Earth, where God/I, himself, sits at the apex of the Lord's Nation!

I am more than a mere man as I carry the testimony of Jesus Christ! Which combines my Human Half with my Godly Half, manifesting a bright light that illuminates both the greater light for the day and the lesser light for the night. My brightened light can be seen as a "Supernova."

The Earth views a Supernova as an extremely large explosion of a star. This stage occurs during the dying days of a star. The star's explosion creates light billions of times brighter than the Earth's "sun" and has enough energy to outshine the galaxy.

The Spiritual comparison unto "Supernova" displays Jesus/I as being the light of the world. I have the stars within my right hand with the power of the Lord's two-edged sword, which flows through my mouth. Given God's explosive power, I am the Spiritual Supernova, allowing the colossal-sized bang that shines brighter than the sun to shine in my strength as the

Son. *(Revelation 1:16)*

I shall teach all how to manifest the spirit of God, which consists of Jesus residing at the depths of every human heart. In order for any human to reach Spiritual freedom, it requires the death of the current spirit; one must harken to my voice as the sound of many waters flowing through the floodgates of Heaven. *(Revelation 1:15)*

Upon the death of one's own spirit, a Holy one shall be gifted unto them which bears a righteous spirit from my Heavenly Father, known as the Holy Spirit.

He who has the Son, too, has the Father, which means every human comes with the first two of the required 3. (The Father, The Son). To complete the trinity, which entails the Holy Spirit, one must completely Spiritually acknowledge and take Spiritual measures to ensure their place in the kingdom of Heaven, which shall first be obtained on Earth, is secure. *(Matthew 18:18-20)*

(Matthew 18:18-20) `

"Assuredly, I say to you, whatever you bind on earth will be bound in heaven, and whatever you loose on earth will be loosed in heaven."

(1 John 2:23)

"Whoever denies the Son does not have the Father either; he who acknowledges the Son has the Father also."

(Colossians 2:6)

"As you therefore have received Christ Jesus the Lord, so walk in Him."

(Colossians 2:3)

"In whom are hidden all the treasures of wisdom and knowledge."

(2 John 1:12)

"I have much to write to you, but I do not want to use paper and ink. Instead, I hope to visit you and talk with you face to face, so that our joy may be complete."

(Revelation: 1:14-15)

14.) *"His head and hair were white like wool, as white as snow, and his eyes like a flame of fire."*

15.) *His feet were like fine brass, as if refined in a furnace, and his voice as the sound of many waters."*

16.) *He had in His right hand seven stars, out of his mouth went a sharp two-edged sword, and His countenance was like the sun shining in its strength."*

(1 Peter 3:4)

"Rather *let it be* the hidden person of the heart, with the incorruptible *beauty* of a gentle and quiet spirit, which is very precious in the sight of God."

Healing-Faith.Org

30

SPIRITUAL NIGGA!

A Spiritual Nigga is a Dark Hue Being who has accepted their Spiritual divined powers from my Heavenly Father. The black person understands that they are the beacons of the world, given their trials and tribulations on the earth's realm. The mere fact that many humans thought it was ok to shun an entire race of people, given their carbonated skin, is ungodly and quite frankly laughable, as those same shunned individuals are indeed the light that appears dark, given their dark outer skin.

The colored people's underlying frustrations are simple: they internally possess the Spirit of my Heavenly Father but get treated less than by those who are genuinely less than spiritually.

Unlike the world view of less than, which lacks worth. The Spiritual meaning of less than implies hierarchy. The blacks are the beacons, and everyone else is less than them, implying that everyone shall follow God's chosen children of Israel. The Dark Hue Spiritual niggas were and are delivered by God for human survival and eternal life.

The colored folks also were previously named Hebrews and Israelites. They were called Hebrews before the conquest of the Land of Canaan, and then the term Israelites came along. The modern term for God's chosen people is the "Colored People," who are too from the tribe of Judah.

Exodus 19:6: "And you shall be to Me a kingdom of priests and a holy nation." These are the words which you shall speak to the children of Israel."

The Spiritual Specimen, also known as an African American, sits above all other worldly terms, including the derogatory term "Nigger", which implies a black person's inability to read or adequately comprehend. Upon the completion of this passage by any colored person, they shall soar beyond the racist and hateful term, Nigger, as they successfully have read, unlike back in the day when the term originated. The Racial Slur suppresses the inner God within every Dark Hue Being. The moment the wording "Nigger" is uttered, it fills hate within the heart of the Gods, which bears anger and rage. The irony is if you alter your thought process on that word, it shall not have a hold on you, nor shall it offend you.

Furthermore, if you apply Spiritual Nigga in front of their insult, it shall satisfy God, who is also of color, as black includes every color, and we all know that God resides within everything. Therefore, any attempt to insult a God shall allow my Heavenly Father to spiritually ignite, which manifests his only begotten son, Jesus, internally from the depths of all hearts. If the insulter is unfamiliar with what a Spiritual Nigga is, well then, one can only assume he has or cannot read, which implies their own ignorance, beyond the sights of my Heavenly Father.

The reason the term, nigger, shall not offend any person of color any longer is that when a disturbed person says, Nigger, in an attempt to insult someone, all God's saints shall say, Spiritual Nigga! Which implies acceptance of being chosen by God. The disturbed person either will reply with something which allows you to display the nine fruits of your heart in your explanation of what a Spiritual Nigga is, or the person's face and mind will fill with confusion, as their aged tactic, better known as child's syndrome, does not bear much effect on the hearts of God's chosen people any longer.

Child Syndrome is when a person has not reached the core of their heart, which is where my Heavenly Father resides. I know the person is not a believer of my Heavenly Father because once a person has reached the depths of their hearts, they begin to speak from the nine fruits of their hearts, which are of an endearing nature. Furthermore, they will understand that the Spirit of Jesus has returned, and the "Host of the Spirits" is a black man, again! Along with understanding that those who have been suppressed for 400+ years are just a repeat in history from the Book of Exodus, also within the Book of Geneses, God tells Father Abram that his descendants will be in a foreign land and serve them and they will be afflicted for 400 years.

So, let's place this story from Exodus in modern Spiritual times; if slavery started around 1619, the year is now 2024, we, as blacks, have been captive longer than God allowed our ancestors to be. The Israelites, who are our ancestors, were in captivity for 400 years, while we, as their descendants, are at 405 years and continuing to count, as blacks are far from the freedom that my Heavenly Father has stored for them in Heaven.

After reading this spiritual scroll, no God of Dark Hue descent shall allow the word nigger to offend them; if they do, I advise them to pray for clarity coupled with reading the Book of Life, known as the Bible. Doing so shall bring Spiritual Understanding to who the dark-hue-skinned individuals are within Heaven's realm.

God resides within the hearts of all believers, as color does not determine entry into Heaven; it solely determines who God chose to lead all others into Heaven. A beacon attracts all others in the form of a blinking light, which indicates a location. The black's genetic makeup from God allows them a form of light within their untainted heart. Their light, which is too the light of Jesus, emits Spiritual rays that all others shall catch with an attempt to ride the frequency to Heaven. All righteous humans are worthy of entry into Heaven; I am just bringing understanding unto the hierarchy of God and his chosen people, whom the world previously hated on.

Genesis 15: 13-14: "Then He said to Abram: "Know certainly that your descendants will be strangers in a land that is not theirs, and will serve them, and they will afflict them four hundred years. 14 And also the nation whom they serve I will judge; afterward they shall come out with great possessions.""

The word Nigga too is used as a friendly gesture amongst friends. The word, nigger, offends, while the word Nigga bears Spiritual understanding, which can be seen by genuine laughter or a welcoming aura.

Although the word may be used by many others who aren't black, a specific internal power only goes for any decent of black and the stragglers who fled Exodus with their God, Moses. The stragglers consist of no one actual color; they are merely followers of Christ who have been awaiting my return. A straggler is someone who becomes separated from their group; there is no disrespect intended within this message, just historical facts.

So, for all others who are not dark in melanin, either you are the people we were running from back in the Egyptian days of Exodus, or you too are God's selected people who smartly chose to follow the Israelites during their journey into the promised land.

The journey that took the Israelites through the desert, towards the Red Sea. So, if anyone has an issue with the status of the blacks and what my Heavenly Father chose, they may need to reconsider their heart, as they are either with us, Spiritual Niggas! or against us, Spiritual Niggas!

With us entails a human knowing and accepting God's chosen people while being against my Heavenly Father and I entail man's disobedience, just like at the beginning of time.

Exodus 12:37-38: "Then the children of Israel journeyed from Rameses to Succoth, about six hundred thousand men on foot, besides children. A mixed multitude went up with them also, and flocks and herds--a great deal of livestock."

For all those who cannot accept God's bestowed powers, please, again, Pray in my name, Jesus! Read the Bible, and this time, review the history of blacks and their continued slavery, then tell me how your heart feels afterward. The reason for their internal power is simple: the more a human is suppressed before their Spiritual flame, the more Spiritual Power the flame comes with. The blacks have been suppressed for 400+ years, which bears a mountain of Godly power among the masses.

The Blacks have endured far more than any other race, previously or currently, as our struggle remains. Their death toll is higher than any other race, given the lack of reparations for their so-called freedom in 1863, which marked the official year of freedom known as the Emancipation Proclamation. Their lack of guidance is due to them losing their way from God, who is the source of their spiritual flame. The source of all humanity has arrived to Spiritually lead all God's people, chosen or otherwise.

How can any nation claim freedom if said nation uses false gods idolized as money to suppress their people? The money system operates in many ways, one being nepotism for sure as if a human child bears wealthy parents, friends, or lovers for they themselves are rich, earned or otherwise.

This poor tactic sometimes ensures wealth in the hands of the wrong people for generations to come, no matter how much blood was shed over the money. Natural resources are accessible from God, so why should God's people pay for the free resources, such as food and shelter, provided by the same trees that give humans oxygen? Shall the trees charge humans for their contribution unto the world? I can assure you that no human has enough to repay anything my Heavenly Father created for their pleasure.

How does an American Indian/Native American get 9 thousand dollars a month, free education, and private land for their ancestor's struggles? But the African Americans/Black Americans continue to live in poverty and receive nothing for their current struggles or their ancestor's struggles? There is only one true logical answer to the question.

The King of Kings has arrived. I am the Messiah who has come to restore world order and fight for the reparations for the blacks, as the same railroads they built are still being occupied. I am sure that all would understand why I, being of Godly nature, would want the same equality as the American Indians; after all, they were beaten, killed, and tortured for their land. The only difference between them and us is that America stole their land while enslaving the blacks to build onto the stolen land. But don't forget, we were also stolen from our land.

The American Indians deserve all they receive, plus more. But so do the African Americans.

I, Christ! I shall restore spiritual power within my people of color and all righteous people. I shall be the Spiritual Being who brings forever change unto the earth's realm, as I offer enlightenment unto the hearts of all my Spiritual Niggas, who have awaited my return.

31

BRUSHEE'S KEEPER!

God's love becomes plentiful to those who genuinely believe in his existence. The presence of God can be shown through a painting parable. I will describe how God controls my life, given that I am a recipient of the Holy Spirit.

God is the painter, for I am the paintbrush. The portrait entails abstract imagery as I, being the brush, have the ability to influence what's being painted, given my choices within the earth's realm. The painting is still made perfect as true beauty is felt by the heart rather than viewed by human sight. Although the initial view compliments the collaboration of colors, once a more profound meaning of the portrait is given or observed by either the brushee or the brushee's keeper, is when heartfelt understanding occurs. For I am the brushee, and my Heavenly Father is my keeper. Therefore, my Heavenly Father can be known as "Brushee's Keeper," which entails God sitting high, painting my life on a blank canvas. While God sits on his throne/Seat, with his paintbrush (I), in his right hand. (Matthew 16: 14-20), The drawings and colors are added based on my life's choices, or lack thereof. Therefore, ultimately, my choices dictate the completeness of my portrait.

In front of my Heavenly Father is a blank canvas on a painting stand. The full color of the canvas is dark hue, as it depicts my skin color (Revelation 1:12-16).

Immediately surrounding God's area, on all sides, are several incomplete portraits scattered about, faintly showing imagery of my entire life, past, present, and future. Some fallen portraits are incomplete because every time I blatantly sin, my decision stops the painter from continuing his Perfectly imperfect portrait. While other fallen portraits entail my future sins that the painter has already forgiven. (Matthew 12: 31-32) (1 John 1:9).

As I begin to pray, as the Holy Bible suggests (Matthew 6:6), my Heavenly Father forgives me of all my sins, given my genuine repentance unto his desires, of course.

I then begin to manifest the Spiritual light which shines for others to view. The earth needs the sun for survival, just as humanity needs the Son of Man, I. (John 8:12)

The completed piece of art is imperfect in their sight, but from the inner workings of things, that imperfection shall always cause me growth as without submitting to the painter, it will cause a mass of incomplete portraits.

Allow my Heavenly Father (Painter/Keeper) to create a perfectly imperfect portrait of his children (Paintbrush/brushee), as beauty bears more illumination when the portrait is complete.

32

HEIR TO THE THRONE!

This passage will entail the continued struggle of any person who physically harms an Anointed Human Being.

Beyond physical harm, this passage will also describe the generational curses linked to such a foolish decision to even think of harming a child created in God's image. Furthermore, if any person speaks blasphemy on the Son of Man, Markais Ruben. C Neal Sr, their fate will be sealed within the kingdom, as the only way to enter "Heaven" is through the Son, who is I, Markais Ruben. C Neal Sr!

It works just like this: If the Son, who is also known as the "Messiah," is denied his throne, within the heart or mind of any human, given their lack of belief unto my Heavenly Father's gift unto the world, which is believing that his chosen anointed Son, Christ! has returned to free the hearts and minds of all righteous believers. Then, the "Lamb of God!" will not be at the ultimate height of his emotions, which is Love, which, too, is my Heavenly Father, nor will he be at the ultimate peak of his feelings, which is Peace, which too is Heaven. Given such disgrace, the human half of him will be unable to clearly compre-hend or discern the heart and mind of his adversary, which is God's nemesis. The Godly half of him will wonder why any human would instead choose a worldly god over my Heavenly Father, who has provided the "Book of Life"

(Bible) as a resource for all humans to learn who I AM! Many former prophets have spoken about my return to the earth's realm. They, too, were humans created in the image of God, as he speaks through his most remarkable creations.

My mere identity is the Spirit of Love, which shall guide all humanity to sit at the right hand of my Heavenly Father. I shall Spiritually guide everyone who genuinely believes I, Jesus Christ, has returned to the earth's realm.

If a human being does not believe in the "Author and Finisher of our Faith, "which is "I AM," or attempts to do physical, mental, or emotional harm to any chosen child, the deception unto my Heavenly Father, shall bear many curses, not only unto their lives, but the lives of their family members, their friends, or the friends of their friends. Let's go a little deeper in case some do not have ears and cannot hear my message.

If I, Markais Ruben. C Neal Sr, or Markais Neal Jr, or any member of my Heavenly Father's gang is harmed, they first immediately enter Spiritual Heaven, where the Spirit soars after a righteous death beyond earth. The reason is simple; they have already obtained the Holy Spirit, which is currently allowing them Heaven on earth. Secondly, the trader, which shall succumb at their own demise, shall cause ruination combined with damnation unto many seeds on earth, living or otherwise, directly involved or otherwise.

It is now time for every human to begin caring for one another as the actual image of my Heavenly Father involves all his children. We as humans have the ability to feel my Heavenly Father, who is always near, as his presence within your heart allows for his Spiritual thoughts into your mind, which creates God himself as he shall be seen through his newly ordained vessel sighted through their works unto him, which are embedded on their hearts, and shown on their actual faces. When they smile, you are viewing God's smile. When they eat, you view God eating as his Spirit resides in all things, faithful or otherwise.

Does anyone remember when my Heavenly Father destroyed every human but the remaining eight, which were Noah and his wife, Sham, Ham, Japheth, and their wives? Let's say that the sequence of events will not happen by water, nor will the names of the ones remaining be the same.

I can only imagine fire from an impactful event. In the theory of fire, I can only think of a few things of possibility for the planet Earth. My research on Google says that if the Sun dies, "it will evolve into a bloated red giant, gobbling up mercury and Venus, and scorching the earth."

This Spiritual parallel is very simple to the Holy Spirit.

Given that the Holy Spirit has no sight until a human inhabits it, If I hear (auditory means) what Google is saying, which is what I placed in quotes, I then hear Son instead of Sun. Therefore, I can only bring credence unto both, as me being the Son of Man, and the tangible sun, being the light that Earth needs to sustain life, and if either star does not sustain life, well, reread the quotes again or just research in google, "What will happen if the sun dies, then everyone shall understand my parable, as I am the "King of Parables."

On a more positive note, suppose a person has accepted their God-given power, treasures stored no further than their own clear heart and mind. In that case, they become a human created in God's image, and their lineage shall bear good fruit, as the Spirit of God shall dwell with their many generations to come.

If a person does not accept their God-given power, they will be like a rotten tree, bearing sour fruit and lacking rich leaves. Their Spiritual stunt in growth is because of their malnutrition of the Son of man's words.

Here is another parable for the Sun and the Son through photosynthesis.

Facts about a tree and required sunlight: Just like a tree within the world requires energy from the sunlight, as it bears nutrition unto their leaves, allowing them to create their own food. Every plant requires its own level of sunlight, as all plants are different; even those from the same family bear different fruits amongst their likeness.

If it lacks sunlight, it fails to produce chlorophyll, which creates the green pigment in plants. Additionally, the plant turns pale through different hues of deterioration. It becomes "leggy," meaning stems become long and thin and appear to be reaching toward the source of the light, which is the Sun.

If the tree bears too much Sun, it can go through a phase called Sunscald, which often damages its overall health, from the bark to the leaves and fruit.

But, if the tree gives enough sunlight back to the source, it can retain its proper absorption amount. The light energy, which is gathered from the Sun, will be converted into chemical energy, which is stored within the glucose molecules. Tiny organelles called chloroplasts, which store the energy of sunlight, are inside the plant cell.

Science only takes you so far, then comes God! ¬ – Nicholas Sparks.

Here are facts about the Tree of Life, which the Son of Man gives:

Genesis 3:22: "Then the LORD God said, "Behold, the man has become like one of Us, to know good and evil. And now, lest he put out his hand and take also of the tree of life, and eat, and live forever."

The time has now come as the tree of life has been protected and guarded as our Heavenly Father commanded. Take now and live forever as God's promise unto the world has come to fruition, allowing the Holy Spirit, which rests within his chosen Son, Markais Ruben. C Neal Sr. The feat that allowed for a man to be created from the dust of the ground, contextual for smoke, and breathed into his nostrils, the breath of life, contextual for inhaling and exhaling the tree of life through my nasal cavity, allowing me to see the workings of God, amid total submission unto his power. No more shall the tree of life be guarded as the Holy Spirit has broken through the firmament and will guide planet Earth amid their spiritual expedition.

Just as all humans within the earth's realm require the Love of my Heavenly Father, also known as the tree of life, they must put out their hands and take also of the tree of life, and eat, and live forever.

I shall provide the spark of life into the limbs of all righteous believers, which provides greenery, also known as the "food of life," unto any human belonging to my Heavenly Father. As the Son, I shall allow every righteous human to drink from the cup of my fellowship, which too is the fellowship of our Father, who art in Heaven. I shall water those who are thirsty from the water used in correlation with the Sun as it floods on the dry ground.

If a human lacks the food of life, their spiritual diet shall starve them to death. Death shall come as it did for Adam at the beginning of time, which entails death within the Spirit, which still allows for a human to occupy a space on earth, but within the sights of my Heavenly Father, that human too is known as an empty vessel, who is showing praise to the wrong God, as the Love of our Lord, Jesus Christ! may be removed from their existence, marking them as "godless children" referring to children without a God that my Heavenly Father spoke about in the "Book of Hosea", placing them under worldly commands as opposed to Godly commands.

Being the Son of Man, I shall, too, create photosynthesis for the dark hue community, as their Hebrew king has arrived, to provide their souls with enough Son light for their Spiritual inner strength to manifest, which shall entail their resurrection date and a new Spiritual identity.

I shall manifest the Holy Spirit of Jesus Christ within all believers, but for sure within the section of the community who has suffered and prayed within my name for the last 400 plus years, as the beginning of slavery was around the 1619s, which places us strictly at 405 from years from date.

If history repeats itself? Why has Dark Hue been enslaved longer than our ancestors, even after my heavenly Father advised 400 years? Now, with low wages, inadequate housing, and a struggling education system. I can't forget about our price range for health care.

I can only come up with one solution when many humans say they know my God; they are not uttering words about my Heavenly Father if a human knows our Lord, Jesus Christ! Then, Love shall dwell within the hearts for the chosen people, which are the dark hue individuals.

Revealing that the dark hue community is God's chosen people, just as the Hebrews or Israelites were before, does not imply that any other Hue is less than; it simply sheds light on the mere facts about my Heavenly Father's Spiritual Hierarchy.

This statement shall reach the masses, who shall pray for the Spiritual gifts of Knowledge, Understanding, and Wisdom.

Here is why the Dark Hue population has been chosen as beacons by God.

Within the Spirit, colors mean nothing, but since within planet Earth it signifies so much; It was used as a way of revealing a form of struggle that creates a different type of human being, as dealing with racism is a constant battle that is fueled by foolish man and not brought to attention by my Heavenly Father.

Furthermore, the dark hue community has been and is still being restrained by merely their pigment instead of the totality of their circumstance.

Along with God, which is Love, shall be understanding of the fact that Christ! Walked and was sent to uplift and guide his Hebrew community. Upon departing, all knew the Spirit would return.

In the 13th century BC, God used Moses as God to his people to uplift the Israelites from underneath the thumb of the pharaoh.

I, being the Son of Man, also known as the second coming of Christ! have come to liberate my Dark Hue community from under the thumbs of those who control their low wages or the ones who provide them with poor housing infrastructure systems, or the ones who charge blacks for education but give Native Americans free education as if their struggle somehow trumps our 405-year struggle. One thing we can all agree on is at least the Native Americans received something from America, who were known as, and still are known as, Godless children. I.E., the governmental entities and their deceit.

Do the chosen people get our reparations now? Here is why I ask, and I say there is always time. During any catastrophe where many lives are taken or altered, we, as "America," fork out billions for the cause. Rightfully so.

My Heavenly Father has declared me to be the Son of Man in the Sunshine State of Florida, which shall shine in my strength. May I speak on behalf of my people for the promises that God, being Jesus Christ, has risen me for?

Isaiah 44: 8: "Do not fear, nor be afraid; have I not told you from that time and declared it? You are My witnesses. Is there a God besides Me? Indeed, there is no other Rock; I know not one."

I am your Lord, Jesus Christ!

My Father and I, given we are one, names are located on all currencies within the United States.

What God is the United States referring to? GOD, meaning Yahweh! /YHWH! /Jesus Christ! or another God, printed on something that many humans idolize. The response will be felt when I, as the owner, by name, of the actual money, ask for it in reparations for my struggling Dark Hue community.

The prodigal Son has returned to claim my throne!

Isaiah 44: 1-8

1 Peter 2:9: "But you are a chosen generation, a royal priesthood, a holy nation, His own special people, that you may proclaim the praises of Him who called you out of darkness into His marvelous light;"

Revelation 1:16: "He had in His right hand seven stars, out of His mouth went a sharp two-edged sword, and His countenance was like the sun shining in its strength."

Genesis 3:22: "Then the LORD God said, "Behold, the man has become like one of Us, to know good and evil. And now, lest he put out his hand and take also of the tree of life, and eat, and live forever.""

Matthew 6:9-13: In this manner, therefore, pray:

"Our Father in heaven, Hallowed be Your name. 10 Your kingdom come. Your will be done

On earth as it is in heaven.

11 Give us this day our daily bread. 12 And forgive us our debts,

As we forgive our debtors.

13 *And do not lead us into temptation, But deliver us from the evil one.*

For Yours is the kingdom and the power and the glory forever. Amen."

33

YAHWEH'S SON, JESUS CHRIST!

The Western Wall/The Wailing Wall/ The Buraq Wall

God's "Healing Faith Organization" Western Wall Prayer

The Temple Mount, also known as Haram al-Sharif, al-Aqsa Mosque compound.

. . .

On previous page:

The Western Wall, also known as the Wailing Wall, is one of the most sacred places within The Holy City of Jerusalem, along with Temple Mount. Prayers are made, submitted, and inserted into the Western wall for Holy Heaven Consideration.

My Heavenly Father and his angels advised all humans
That I was Spiritually Coming,
Onto the streets I go, chasing and running down God's resurrected angels as I come riding a horse, camel, or hat strapped onto a donkey.

Or, unto the black stereotype, I shall be swinging like a monkey,
Spiritually back and forth from Heaven and Earth,
Enlightened grace unto my dome, accepting thy Godly power like a Heavenly orientated Spiritual junkie.

Within my hands, feet, and even unto my knees,
As a human drops down, brought forth Heaven above hell, faithfulness unto thy righteous fruit-bearing tree.

Within God's Temple, Within God's Footstool,
I, AM, Jesus Christ, the head rabbi of my Heavenly Father's Spiritual rules, unto thy earthly School
I AM thy Heart; I have arisen from the Heavens above,
Resurrected with the treasured Holy Spirit inside, like the purity of a taintless, soaring, fearless lion and dove.

A second chance involves a human following after Jesus Christ, which is me,
Christ's inner Identity, delivered for the start of the afterlife, which shall set all

other children Eternally free, but only with sights unto Heaven shall one be permitted to Spiritual see.
Within thy righteous bearing fruit shall a child of God know,
Implying those with an ear to listen as God himself is here, within thy open Heart, mind, and Soul, I shall bestow, too, implying a chosen child being led into the firmament, unto the earthly Things they overcome and outgrow.

To those who knock, open, and then enter.
Inner Spiritual enlightenment that all once knew, bringing forth God's Holy Spirit for grace to remember.

Within thy womb, within God's Holy house,
Within thy entire divined wholeness-details, God's Holy Tabernacle spread throughout.
As the Tabernacle is with men, and I shall be their God,
I come Spiritually and tangibly, as God's Holy Spirit is embedded into a righteous man on earth, while my mind, Heart, and soul reside Heavenly abroad.

Deep within thy Heart, even deeper within thy mind,
Astral project into Heaven, it's quite the opposite; although Heaven and Earth are parallel, the Worldly hate is due to foolish man's design.

Escape from earthly trauma, escape thy worldly prison,
Manifest thy light from deep within, God's precision grace you shall feel, the presence of your Lord God, implying belief that I, Christ Jesus, have indeed risen.

As I stand strictly on business within the nature of God,
Yahweh's son Jesus has returned, do rejoice with an open hearted applaud.

34

THE KINGDOM AT HAND

JOHN 3:3:

"Jesus answered and said to him, "Most assuredly, I say to you, unless one is born again, he cannot see the kingdom of God."

Luke 17:21:

"Nor will they say, 'See here!' or 'See there!' For indeed, the kingdom of God is within you."

To be born again is to turn away from thy past wicked ways,
Manifesting the light of God, which is within you,
Heavenly kingdom, unto God's Heavenly delivered son, and his walkable path,
known as the son providing sun rays.

Unto thy healing faith coupled with the genuine belief that Jesus would return someday,
I, Christ Jesus, have arrived, Holy streaming light, illuminated feet unto God's Heavenly runway.

Even within your lane, I, Jesus Christ, shall show you,
The meaning of your worldly struggle, Spiritual inheritance unto all things righteous humans grow through.

Are you righteously chosen, are you Spiritually selected,
Are you able to obtain entrance into the kingdom, seeing beyond your worldly sight, relying on My Heavenly Father for what's next, implying you knew Heaven was coming as your open heart Suggested or, furthermore, expected.

Unto the Love of God shall I inject and erect,
Spiritual growth within thy seed, as I AM King
Thy heart longs for and even before have we met,
Are you awaiting something for your tangible sight,
or is the Kingdom of Heaven within you, delivered among my Heavenly Father's provisions, as I, Jesus Christ, shall provide envision using God's Spiritual might.

I AM the Son of God, and I complete the package of what the world needs, My Heavenly Father has given me an oath,

That I must uphold, unto his right hand, did my heavenly heart accept,
implying I righteously sat and openly agreed.

Within his throne is where my heart and mind openly sit,
Unto his throne does God's love openly reward, as his chosen son, where and to
whom shall I Gift and spiritually permit,
Unto his throne shall I give inner insight,
The height of Heaven shall shine rays for open, lifted guidance, as I possess
God's Holy Spirit, Therefore, a Darkened knight, with night vision or inner lit
vision like a bright streetlight.

Exalted ability unto the gift of life,
Slicing and cutting through trauma,
Holy delivered grace, even unto the crumbs which have fallen from the likes of
my bread knife.

Unto thy last supper, as this is my second and finally coming, I shall exalt
God's chosen children While mentally crucifying those who adore Spiritual
conduct unbecoming.

That is determined when a human does something against my Heavenly
Father's will,
Within their chosen destruction is what I shall openly Attack, devour, and
righteously kill.

Kill them with lovable words and gestures of kindness,
Astral projection, aerial view, giving them a taste of their own medicine,
opening their view even unto their own inner blindness.

Will their heart sustain them, will they make it through?

My Heavenly Father forgave Judas,
But Judas couldn't forgive Judas; what shall one with such massive sin do,
My Heavenly Father advises everyone to use prayer, so that's what I say,

Identical resurrected Holy Spirit, I AM Jesus Christ, and I have returned,
enlightening attack and Conquering others with Spiritual might along the way.

Worldly relinquishment of all things that are unrighteously worrisome or prob-
lematically hectic.

Placing their heart in my Spiritual Lane,
Shall cause for an open dialogue, unto their open heart shall I, Jesus Christ,
righteous and spiritually test it.

Permitted to judge as God has delivered the Spirit unto the Host,
Heaven is at hand, I AM God's chosen son,
A pillar of light, a beacon within God's Heavenly observation post.

35

——————

HEAVENLY CONSIDERATION!

Saqqara Pyramid (The stepped Pyramid) Memphis, Egypt (Giza Governorate)

Within God's lighthouse, I shall forever shine. The Holy Spirit embedded into a righteous man,
Into God's Temple, implying I AM the son of man, which is divinely aligned.

God is love. Therefore, all humans shall release their hate, pride, and worldly pain,
Within God's realm known as Heaven, I AM the living God and the earth's savior, implying thy Spiritually righteous main vein,
Yahweh has granted his son, Jesus Christ, everlasting and eternal permission,
Dominion over all Heaven and the Earth,
Key Holder of thy afterlife, unto the faithful shall I, the Messiah, grant Heavenly admission.

Within the Kingdom of God, all is forever fair, Within the righteously proud and spiritually worthy,
An honorable awakening shall allow a human to conquer their Spiritual heir.

Claim thy Heavenly prize, claim thy spiritual stake,
Only unto God's chosen shall I manifest the Holy Spirit within, which means,
unto their hearts And minds, shall I righteously Illuminate amid their wake.

Elevation of worldly trauma, held-on pain, and massive hurt,
Liberation unto my sheep, into thy afterlife, shall a human fulfill God's life,
reaping what's been Sown, feeding on Heavenly dessert.

A righteous death implies a human, within their heart, acknowledging my Heavenly Father's existence.

It, too, implies a human believing in me, Jesus Christ, which spiritually leads all humans to the path of least resistance.

Into the air, where else shall a human soul righteously reach,
Individual grace, as faith is solitude, unto each lamb's heart, do I, the King of Kings, openly preach.

When two or more righteous Spirits are gathered together, the Holy Spirit shall thrive,
Become one with yourself after accepting I, Lord God, to resurrect and become forwardly alive.

Once the Holy Spirit freely enters your heart, an aerial liftoff it shall be,
Only through I, the Son of God, shall any human enter Heaven's corridor.

Within my Heavenly Father's consideration, shall one come off the footstool, becoming temple-bound and free.

Once a genuine human evolves into a Spiritual Being, for Heaven bound they shall be,
An angel without disguise, escaping and dodging all earthly unrighteousness at all costs,
regardless of level or degree.

Always be aware of thy human limitations,
On to the afterlife, praying for God's Spiritual, Heavenly consideration.

Exalt beyond the world and all therein, spiritually implying finding, I, Jesus Christ, which is Yahweh's Son, the earth's returned beloved friend.

For sight unto thy Spiritual afterlife liberation, Righteousness among free will,
Without the slightest bit of Godly hesitation,
The Fear of God shall guide all humans righteously straight,
Mocking an upright tree full of righteous fruit, unto the bearing of God's Holy seed,
Shall I reveal a saint of God, open Heavenly Sesame to recreate.

Within their forethought, within thy afterlife, within their foresight,
Shall I guide all of God's angels into Heaven, among consideration to right-eously make Holy and eternally right.

What shall be thy goal other than Holiness and thy aftermath,

Pray for entrance into Heaven, implying acknowledgment and recognition of God's ordained Temple inner-lit craft.

At Yahweh's right hand do I humbly sit, righteously stand, and forever lay,
Within the grace of every righteous prayer, has the Holy Spirit returned within a righteous man to eternally stay.

Within Yahweh's consideration, unto thy human choice,
Within heartfelt healing faith, shall each human deny their flesh amid their heavenly aerial hoist.

Top shelf grace or a secured spot within God's kingdom temple,
The second coming is here. Inner enlightenment, as I shall cast Godly judgment on the reaping-hearted righteous and their mental

As all humans shall reap what they righteously sow,
Imagine me as a Spiritual Godly cupid; unto the entire world shall I aim and pierce with God's Rod, Aka. Perfect lit precision among Cupid's Bow.
Last but not least, please allow the Holy Spirit to overtake thy flesh,
Nor will they say here it is! or there it is!

Heaven is within thy righteous heart, resurrected among thy enlightened mind, connected by the Main vein, implying God's heartbeat under thy inner chest.

Citations:

***Luke: 17: 20-21:**

"Now when He was asked by the Pharisees when the kingdom of God would come, He answered them and said, "The kingdom of God does not come with observation; 21 nor will they say, [a]'See here!' or 'See there!' For indeed, the kingdom of God is [b]within you."

***Psalm 11:**

1. In the LORD I take refuge; how can you say to my soul,

"Flee like a bird to your mountain,

2 for behold, the wicked *a*bend the bow; they have fitted their arrow to the string to shoot in the dark at the upright in heart;

3 if the foundations are destroyed, what can the righteous do?" *1*

4 The LORD is in his holy temple; the LORD's throne is in Heaven;

his eyes see, his eyelids *t*est the children of man.

5 The LORD tests the righteous,

but his soul hates the wicked and the one who loves violence.

6 Let him rain coals on the wicked;

fire and sulfur and a scorching wind shall be the portion of their cup.

7 For the LORD is righteous;

he loves righteous deeds;

the upright shall behold his face.

36

INTO THE CLOUDS I HAVE COME!

Rock Verbiage *Seize the eternal life that has your calling* -Monastery of Saint Simeon

Within the clouds, your King has come,

Inhaling the tree of life, standing upright like vertical leveling known as being plum

Within the THC, derives for a pleasant sight,

Men were created from the dust of the ground,

Breathed into their nostrils, known as God giving them his breath of life.

Vital Spiritual breath like a massive storm,

Blow through tornado destruction,

As I shall break through any barrier to guide my Father's chosen children home,

As clouds are contextual for the dust,

Inhale and exhale,

Within your nostrils shall God's spirit excel and grow; within his will and your freedom shall we all trust.

Particular age, Particular strand,

Do believe that Jesus has returned,

To guide the entire world on unlocking your inner being, implying creation within his Spiritual likeness, identical to I, the son of Man.

Among the once forbidden fruit, which is the bud, raised from the tree,

Spiritual enlightenment, within the depth of my heart, which has captured my mind and set my fulfilled sights, resurrection breakthrough or Heavenly free.

Gifted with the ability to soar within the clouds,

Heaven on earth has arrived,

Mind-blowing prophecies, which shall be openly gifted as they are rewards given aloud.

Miracles for the strong, strength unto the weak,

Having the faith of a mustard seed,

Shall place many humans on the correct Godly

Course, implying Spiritual freedom and movement unto their once coward feet.

Into the clouds, an inner righteous Spiritual being I stand,

Clarity into your forgiving heart and open mind,

Implying, I, Jesus Christ, AM indeed the returned Son of Man, linking identities among God's DNA strand.

I AM the Son of God, also known as the King of Peace,

Into the clouds I have come, providing heavenly armor unto God's chosen, also known as his chosen children and even his Spiritual police.

Into their open heart, can my Heavenly Father see, become a spy for God, allowing for his inner envision, linking the Holy Trinity.

Apply the ceremonial olive oil,

Lubricating all things righteous,

Into the clouds, I have come,

Heaven liberation, Spiritual Peace amid and over any worldly crisis,

I have merely come to fulfill the prophecy in which few humans knew,

Many humans thought they would not see the day that God himself returned to the earth,

God in the flesh, for I AM his living spoken proof.

If your good outweighs your wrong, then you shall be proud that I have come.

If your bad outweighs your good, then you are my Heavenly Father's adversary, spiritually Rejecting thy inner power and wisdom of where your inner might has come from.

If God's inner presence becomes known, a unique token ye shall be,

I Am Jesus Christ, the son of Man, brought forth like Moses; God speaks when a flame of fire burns through the midst of the pleasant burning tree.

I am becoming too aware, even in my sleep,

Spiritual lucid dreams: God is showing out, as I reject hell, what need is there to be discrete.

Full force power, front-forward action,

Within the clouds, Jesus has come,

Clear thy heart and mind to openly accept God's one-on-one Spiritual transaction.

As faith is solitude, it begins with an open heart,

Become faithful to my Heavenly Father,

Accepting his Holy Spirit and his son Jesus as

An Open dialogue is how we shall start.

. . .

Into the clouds I have come, into the clouds all righteous humans shall go,

Reaching into thy heart, locating my Heavenly Father, unto thy good deeds shall a sainted prospect know.

Acknowledge what is within your once-tainted heart and mind,

letting go of all cowardness, Implying forever standing upright, being plum as I have come, Spiritually seeking, and too shall I openly find.

Locating the chosen by their brazen inner identity alone,

Becoming forever courageous, Accepting our Spiritual power as the Holy Spirit places you on God's leveled throne

Judgment day has arrived. May I take a peek into your free will,

Your choices shall determine whether my Heavenly Father's presence is within you, implying Your faith and belief that I, Jesus, the true Lord God, live.

If you Quit, if you surrender,

Consume the tree of life to cast away all judgment, as punishment is solely ours to render.

My Heavenly Father calls the shots, for he has last say over who lives, for I AM the last delivered Lamb,

Sacrificed to ensure that every vessel on earth has the Spiritual ability to evolve and live.

For those who constantly revert or constantly backtrack, I shall withdraw my physical Spiritual presence away from you,

As the Tangible, Son of Man, has finally returned back.

Puff puff away, puff puff pass,

Inheritance unto the Herbs of field,

Implying the clouded tree, before the creation of man and back into their once casted-out spirits,

Thank my God for freedom at last.

I pray for all to adhere;

No more shall any human postpone their destiny,

Praise and rejoice as the Son of God, known as Jesus Christ, is finally here.

On the third day, my Heavenly Father created the field of trees,

Humans were created on the sixth day,

Breathing into their nostrils, a smokable substance embedded with the duplication of God's seed.

A seed within itself is finally for the taking,

No more shall a cherubim be in the way,

As it's legal now, as mental health is taking over,

And shall be Spiritually breaking.

Tearing away many families, given many lack spiritual intelligence,

Or causing a righteous breakthrough for many families among their divined inner inheritance

Mother Earth, the smokeable female part of the cannabis plant,

Pleasant to the sight, laughable envision, and inner charisma, as within their prayer, Jesus shall be the name every human praise and chant.

I Thank God for all three,

The Spiritual Father, I, the Tangible Son, and the Holy Spirit, which is the smoke embedded Within the flame of God's flower, as he speaks from the magical acknowledgment midst of said tree.

Every herb of the field was given for structural healing to meet,

Physical or mental Spiritual enlightenment

Within that particular seed is how one grows beyond oneself, known as having no need to be Spiritually discrete.

Into the clouded sky we all shall go,

As every human shall shout to honor the King, as

One by One, inner enlightenment is like a bed,

I shall provide covers for the chilly snow.

The chills within your heart as every truth shall unfold,

It's time for all righteous humans to stand up as I Spiritually lead the way for the courageous and bold.

Genesis & Revelations (Beginning of Heaven on Earth). Implying life+Death= Heaven/Afterlife.

37

HELL ON EARTH!

Rocket after Rocket,

Missile after missile,

Hell is within those who explosively take innocent lives,

The ones who lack Spiritual prayer, therefore, are determined to ignite their Spiritual dismissal.

Vindication among all their wrongdoing, repenting and giving it to God,

Clearing thy worldly cache is how one drops their human facade.

Understanding and coming to terms with everything they have done,

Divine sunlight, like the vision given by God, identical grace like the rays from his son.

Within my dark hue image, the shine is for sure to appear bright,

The combining of all colors and things,

I AM the light at the end of the tunnel,

Sighted among Heaven's sought after light.

Within my heart, all of God's chosen children shall be free, placing aside all rockets and missiles that are polluting the air,

Affecting the issues pertaining to global warming.

My Heavenly Father advised everyone I was coming, Unto the hearts and minds of the wicked, My Heavenly prayer is for them all to stop their unrighteous succumbing.

If anyone wants to take their own life, then screw unto you fool,

Do not take others with you or even yourself,

Doing any one of the two shall cause a break in the chain of God's heaven-entering rules.

A screw must be loose within their head, for I have come to Spiritually fill the holes of any Foolish human with or without sights on how to obtain the righteous Heaven ahead.

Every human alive calls for a particular Spiritual task,

Stop being a Spiritual inner robber, concealing God's identity, rejecting his inner likeness, hiding behind their worldly mask.

The flesh of humans was for sure to corrupt the world,

No more do-overs,

As becoming a righteous being,

Providing our love is how one gains knowledge within the delightful referral.

A reference from God's chosen Son, Jesus,

Upon stepping away from sin, implying all unrighteous thoughts and acts known as Spiritually being egregious

Within the pits of hell, many reject their power to soar,

Running from even thy own truth, which is

Suppressed in the midst of thy corroded inner hell bearing core.

Hell on Earth is the current state of war,

Spiritual warfare, or world war,

Bomb, missile, or gun, the same surface foolishness as countless times before.

The Humans who did not believe or, furthermore, the ones who assumed it was over,

Lacking Heaven on Earth, I AM your Lord God, Known as Jehovah!

I AM The Lion of the Tribe of Judah known as Kais da Beast,

I have come to devour and deliver on God's promised Heavenly feast.

Within your food of thought shall I eat,

Bloody redemption, unto my Heavenly Father's heartbeat

Within your open and bloody heart shall take a peek

It won't be that difficult, given even within yourself, it's too myself, Jesus, as all hearts shall openly seek.

Does the blood taste familiar, and is the meat rare? I AM a jealous God; stay back away from my prey, implying those who pray, you've been warned; please be Heavenly aware.

38

ULTIMATE SPIRITUAL WISDOM

Jerusalem, Israel- overlooking the only closed gate, out of the 8, which surrounds the Old of Jerusalem built in the 16th Century.

We are one, as I possess the Holy Spirit; please open thy righteous heart to undeniably receive us.

To know my Heavenly Father is to know he Had a divined son,

The one who died on the cross and rose regardless of the men outside the sealed tomb, as within said death, God had already ordained and won.

To know my Heavenly Father Yahweh is to know he Has a righteous son,

Risen and delivered a graceful human, as I AM Jesus Christ, highly resurrected as the beloved chosen one.

Within God's choice, within my Spiritual acceptance and Heavenly plea,

Within my righteous promise, has our Heavenly Father ordained and gifted Spiritual gifts unto me.

Consider me a gold token of Heavenly Appreciation and Godly Love,

Consider my Heavenly Father, the Spiritual slot machine, from those who sit at his right hand, pulling the lever for treasure from above.

Pull thy lever, roll thy dice, or spill thy tea,

Coughing up all thy truth is the only way to grow Into a Spiritual Being to become Heavenly appetizing and free.

With my Heavenly Father as thy food source and I, Jesus, as thy soft drink, loving grace shall Pour quicker than any human can think, drink, or blink.

Within a wink or blink of thy eye, I advised all I was soon to come,

Within the belief that I have indeed arrived, shall cause for thy brain and heart to become divinely num.

Only for a brief moment as thy heart thaws among thy resurrection, Becoming completely aware of God's Heavenly Hearted visual perception.

Within thy third eye, inside a righteous human and their Holy free will,

Unto a righteous stroke of life, shall God's treasure begin to flow, mocking the action of a Spiritually lever-operated hand mill.

O, and by the way, if I come around and a human can't see or understand what I say, Then, by all means, has that human missed out on their supposed to be Spiritual day.

I AM the Son of Man, and I command all respect upon our Spiritual dialogue,

I possess God's Holy Spirit, implying I AM his walking tabernacle synagogue.

Light on my feet as a feather, given thy repentance of all former sins,

Exalted beyond the earth, pass the scale of justice, into Heaven I AM!, tangibly on earth to Righteously judge and guide others in.

Combing the Ankh of life, with the cross of death,

Shall deliver God's lamb your way, manifesting Spiritual gifts with the double-edged sword, Which is spoken with Yahweh's Holy breath.

Are you a believer in God, and do you follow the likings of Jesus Christ, did you believe within your heart that I would return to bring inheritance among even thy own sacrifice?

Within God's wisdom, within God's Spiritual might,

I AM God in the flesh, sent to brighten thy Spiritual Heavenly light.

I pray for all humans to Spiritually catch my drift, Yahweh is my Father, and I AM his son, Jesus Christ, Heavenly truth, implying we are not a myth.

Within every Holy breath and within all nutritional intake,

Within the tree of life, shall all sins begin to go, implying unrighteousness shall all saints forever mitigate.

As a righteous and Holy child shall always and forever be free, Inner enlightenment unto the depth of their heart,

Implying the third eye, attached unto thy penal gland to divinely and Heavenly see.

For those who urge to find, a human must first righteously seek; within the righteous and Unrighteous shall my Spiritual discernment take an enlightening, hopeful delightful peek.

Within every free will choice and within every free will decision,

I AM your Lord God, as I spiritually stand above any and all earthly religions.

I shall solely conquer with my Heavenly Father's Spiritual gifts,

Unto his Spiritual wisdom shall I redeem all humans, righteousness among entering Heaven, Fully satisfied with no need to drift.

Maintaining thy own Spiritual Lane, no matter thy worldly pain,

Within the righteously spirited, shall I obtain, as within the depths of their heart and soul, shall their mind and double-edged sword openly proclaim.

I have come for removal of thy shoes, placing the worthy on Holy ground,

leading and following God's righteous saints, as God has uplifting angels, also known as Beacons of light, all around

If I, being Jesus Christ, Follow Yahweh's commands, which lead all humans into the highly Sought Spiritually hearted land,

Why, then, would a human not adhere,

Among their free will choice, shall they wholeheartedly believe that Lord Jesus has appeared.

Upon acknowledgment, every child can become saved,

Within God's Ultimate Wisdom and power have I returned amid world war, in which foolish men continue to pave.

Within their sour behavior, within their false notion of the truth,

I AM your Lord God, which stands above all governmental entities, as within my vessel is God's Holy Spirit-embedded proof.

39

HEAVEN'S SPIRITUAL HOST!

THE WELL WHICH THE HOLY FAMILY DRANK FROM

The Cavern Church, where, Virgin Mary and Christ hid, during their
journey to Egypt. Fleeing Roman persecution. Abu Serga.......Cairo,
Egypt.

As human's worldly traverse, one by one, they travel in an attempt to reach
their Spiritual rebirth.

Throughout the earthly thoroughfare, throughout the walk of sinful shame,

The worthy shall be released of all worldly pain,

Within said grace is the reason the spirit of God has touchdown and came.

Look within my eyes for the light,

The eyes on my face and the scope of my heart provide God's Heavenly
eyesight.

I have been delivered to Spiritually help, combining the flesh with the Holy Spirit, pulley together, like a serpentine belt.

I, Jesus Christ, have returned from around the way,

completing God's cycle of love, which comes full circle, as I shall eternally represent God's Trinity ordained Sunday.

Within manna for life, unto the chosen sabbath day,

within the Israelites' Heavenly freedom, has many prophets foretold my return to bring Heaven unto Earth someday.

Unto the hateful critics,

Within the souls of the unrighteous, we hate it,

my Heavenly Father and I, as he killed everyone but 8, as the waters washed away all sin, implying Heavenly risen and abated.

As in entering Heaven shall cleanse all worldly sins,

I Am Heaven's Spiritual Host, seeking those who need a righteous fruit bearing Spiritual friend.

Please Spiritually acknowledge and understand, as allowed guidance is a must,

Between the might of God's power shall we all exalt, resurrect, and spiritually crush amid Heaven's rewarding trust.

What shall thy hearted treasure bring? How does a heaven-bearing child refrain?

Refrain from sin, refrain from worldly pain,

Too Spiritually refrain from consciously doing the wrong thing.

Within belief in me being thy Heavenly Host,

Unto the sweet waters of Marah, like the free-flowing waters off the Mediterranean coast,

As Moses placed the log into the sour water to make it drinkable and sweet,

God has resurrected his delightful son, unto the sour-hearted do I deplore, as I shall scorch them using their own unrighteous deceit.

To those who unrighteously mourn and worldly hold on,

Upon exalting into my Heavenly realm, shall every missed child or loved one internally respawn ,

Holy Midstful spirits with surroundings of eternal transmitted glow,

Heaven's resurrection as the Holy Spirit never forgets,

As it shall bring forth many faces and conversations from before.

The Holy Spirit has come to resurrect from within,

Completely inside out, Holy manifestation with divine remembrance, as every human was of God before the world, implying righteously and deep down, Spiritually, they have the innate ability to get back in.

Throughout the trauma and even throughout the storm,

Although it's Nation against Nation, all of God's saints shall remain prayerful and calm.

The Holy Book of Life entails said struggles and, eventually, God's ending grace,

In 2 Corinthians 6: verse 16-18, it says, I shall walk among my sheep, and the earth shall be my dwelling place.

Within the righteously chosen shall I, the Son of God, eternally guide and effortlessly show,

Within the unrighteous shall they observe in disbelief, but even still shall God's plentiful gifts manifest and blow,

Blow like the Big Bang theory and/or blow their cardinal mind, as within my inner Holy Spirit, is how earthly humans detach and begin their Heavenly igniting climb.

My Heavenly Father may not come when you humanly want him, But surely he's always on needed spiritual time,

I come charging like a Spiritual bull on God's time to lead, as being born on 4/29/1990 makes me a Taurus, implying a bull is my zodiac sign.

With the acceptance of God's chosen Heavenly Host,

implicates thy heightened glory as within my Healing Faith organization, I shall offer Heavenly seats next to my throne within God's temple, implying our Heavenly footstool watching observation post.

Healing-Faith.org

Citations:

Matthew 24: 6-7:

"And ye shall hear of wars and rumours of wars: see that ye be not troubled: for all these things must come to pass, but the end is not yet. For nation shall rise against nation, and kingdom against kingdom: and there shall be famines, and pestilences, and earthquakes, in divers places. "

2 Corinthians 4: 17-18 :

"For our light and momentary troubles are achieving for us an eternal glory that far outweighs them all. So we fix our eyes not on what is seen, but on what is unseen, since what is seen is temporary, but what is unseen is eternal. "

Luke 17:20-21:

"Now when He was asked by the Pharisees when the kingdom of God would come, He answered them and said, "The kingdom of God does not come with observation; 21 nor will they say, 'See here!' or 'See there!' For indeed, the kingdom of God is within you."

40

HEAVEN IS MY HOME

Heaven is my home, it's where God and I are in command,

I AM God too, just with the little g, as I sit at his right and receive everything second-hand.

Second-hand grace, second coming arrival, God has returned unto his home,

Heaven unto thy earth's revival.

Within God's temple which is my primary home,

Onto earth has God risen to claim ownership of my divided secondary birthstone.

High priestly temple and low earthly footstool,

Both lovable places are controlled and commanded by God, using his two highly divined life rules.

Love my Heavenly Father with all thy mind Body, and Soul,

Implying the heights of heaven and the depths of earth, and unto thy neighbor shall Reciprocated love reveal and manifest a righteous mold.

To those who have gone worldly detached and sin irritates thy soul,

Heavenly home has come for you to enter,

Shedding many tears and all sin, please submerge into God's watering hole placenta.

As the firmament is within the midst of thy waters and overcoming of thy pain,

Please understand that the midst of the waters implies human tears, as one repents for their Sins shall it fall like the heavenly growth of herbs from the rain.

As the rain from Heaven produces growth for all earthly trees,

The Son of God has returned from the same Heaven, spiritually sent for the betterment and rain of all human needs.

Spiritual Peace is within my Heavenly home, Greatest and ultimate feeling of divine love,Emotions in total bliss of sweetness as, I, Jesus Christ have come to reconstruct thy earthly honeycomb.

Within the integrity of an upright human, my Heavenly Father shall reveal his face,

But within the hearts of the wicked have they turned to damnation, within their duplicity and Earthly foolishness do they unrighteously crash and chase.

As they sinful chase, they shall run further and further away from my home,

Honoring thy flesh, and rejecting their Spiritual power, unrighteously sticking out like an orange Kicked over traffic cone.

Although the extremely bright cone has a pointed tip, it's misdirection makes it useless, As the falling of thy cone makes it improperly equipped.

How shall a human know where to go if all the traffic cones fall down,

I say drive-by faith, as God's inner voice now comes with an outer image and outer sound.

Within the Spiritual construction zone, Your Lord God is the commander and Chief,

An orange fallen cone can be seen as a human who is in denial or one in spiritual disbelief.

Again, the fallen orange traffic cone can be seen as a fallen angel or an unrighteous human being,

A human in the wrong lane, implying not believing in, I, Jesus Christ, or my Heavenly Father, Who is the one and only Holy all-seeing.

An upright traffic cone with a reflector is an appointed driven child sent by the creator,

A token and beacon of directional truth,

Like one who gives Holy juice and energy, like The purpose of an alternator.

Just as an alternator charge and replenishes the vehicle's lifeline battery,

I shall Spiritually replenish and recharge all hearts, among thy visual remembering of righteous Or unrighteousness within thy open-hearted gallery.

Within every human choice, within every free-will selection,

Within every spoken word, shall my Heavenly Father hear, among our Spiritual dialogue detection.

Within my Heavenly home have I come to speak with every righteous child, Even unto the unrighteous have I returned for them to Holy reconcile.

There was an absence of sunlight while I was gone,

Now does the light shine, as the Son of God, has returned, as Heaven is my home.

Please righteously adhere, please within thy whole heart shall one obey,

Please spiritually understand my message as the Lion of the tribe of Judah has returned and,

Within said Healing-Faith, is Spiritually about all I, the Son of God, have to openly say.

Matthew 5:45:

"that you may be sons of your Father in heaven; for He makes His sun rise on the evil and on the good, and sends rain on the just and on the unjust."

Proverbs 11:30:

"The fruit of the righteous is a tree of life, And he who wins souls is wise."

Psalms 11

Psalms 113

Ecclesiastes 11:7:

"Truly the light is sweet,

And it is pleasant for the eyes to behold the sun;"

Revelation 22:5:

"There shall be no night there: They need no lamp nor light of the sun, for the Lord God gives them light. And they shall reign forever and ever."

41

GOD'S FLAG AMONGST THE NATION!
(3RD BOOK POEM INSERT)

God's Nation consists of all people, not just those who are citizens of a particular country. All races within the Dark and Light hue community. All walks of life, even those incarcerated. God's

Nation consists of every tangible being walking Planet Earth with a heartbeat. The Heart is where God himself sits, while the beat is what sparks the mind to recognize such grace. God's Nation must consist of people who place God above all things within the world, as God has given all those things for our pleasure. The pleasure of man shall not overtake the deliverance from God. "Let everything that hath breath praise the Lord. Praise ye the Lord. *__(Psalms 150: 6)__*

The earth has grown to 195 countries; all countries have flags that proudly display their existence. But, if we are one Nation under God! Why is there no flag that governs all 195 countries that collectively will honor God? This rhetorical question has a simple answer: collectively, all 195 countries must be on the same page, amongst many things—especially their Spiritual Destiny. Suppose countries fight for resources amongst one another. In that case, they do not understand the concept of brotherly love, as the resources are plentiful and will continue to harvest, just as my Heavenly Father did for Moses and the Israelites as if rained bread for six days, and on the 7th day, God ordained that day to be honored, throughout all genealogies. The Holy 7th day is called the "Sabbath." This day also shows grace unto our Heavenly Father as he created the earth in six days and rested on the 7th. Hence the reason, I AM the 7th child.

How can any elected official of any country speak and not mention our Heavenly Father multiple times? If our Heavenly Father controls his child, that child shall obey and be obedient. With that respect, every conversation shall be honored with grace unto the Almighty God. If someone knows our Heavenly Father, they will speak righteously and give him grace through spoken words and acts of kindness, as God is love.

So, any politician who can speak for several minutes on topics surrounding the betterment of all people, God's people, and does not sincerely mention our Heavenly Father amid all topics shall revisit their hearts. Then, God may not have resurfaced there. If God speaks through his chosen children, why wouldn't he give grace unto himself, which shows his identity and allows more children to believe in his identity? How has America been considered the land of the free if nothing is free? Tons of Americans are struggling as people declare their liberation. God also has provided all housing materials within the earth's structure, so why are so many Americans without homes? Especially those who have fought for the same soil they now use as beds (*Veterans*) (*Retired Police*).

Why are countries killing by the thousands just over land that they themselves will die within? Words from the wise, "Those who profit from evil gains shall themselves be ruined."

There is something called "Generational Curses," which can be transferable to future generations. For example, if we are speaking about slavery days, The Generational Curse transfer can be due to acts of foolishness by their ancestors. The transfer may not be affixed to a person but merely through tangible items from the world that could have been left in an estate, trust fund, or any other form of inheritance. The closer someone gets to God, the sooner they will begin to learn the truth about their history, which sheds light on their inheritance by their ancestors.

Once someone learns the truth, the sin or act lies within their hearts, as the choice is theirs— revealing the learned truth or continuing to conceal their family's secret.

God has chosen a select group of people who have been suppressed for over 400 years. The group of people is known as the *Hebrews/Israelites.*

The group's image has been made a mockery of, along with some seeing a resemblance to apes or monkeys. The group's bondage came around 1619. The group had an iron yoke placed around their necks, wrists, and feet. The group was forced to obey a false master who graciously allowed a piece of the Sabbath day to be honored by the chosen *(Psalms collection)*. The group has been beaten beyond belief and has suffered far more than their counterparts. The group is known as the Blacks. The Negros. The Niggers. The Animals, or any other derogatory name, reveals the image of what John saw in the isle of Patmos on the Lord's Day. The image of Jesus!

The selection should not come as a surprise, given their death toll, past and present struggles, lack of respect given by others and at times unto themselves, and last but not least, God had ordained this prophecy well before the struggle of blacks began, hence the reason the Holy Bible speaks with such accuracy in all tenses.

The blacks are the beacons that God has chosen to lead the world. Do you recall the Story of Moses? In the Story, the Pharaoh ordered all the firstborn males to be killed by casting them in the lake; the midwives were Hebrew women and knew God; therefore, Moses was hidden for three months, placed in a basket, and laid in flags by the river's brink and drifted along the Nile River where Pharaoh's daughter bathed. Moses' Sister rescued him from the waters and suggested he be cared for by a Hebrew nurse. Once Moses became older, he became aware of his Spiritual identity and observed an Egyptian "Smiting" a Hebrew Brethren.

Moses killed the Egyptian and buried him in the sand; Moses feared for his life and departed, where he helped the Priest of "Midian, Jethro," seven daughters gather water. Little did Moses know that one of the women he helped would become his bride, "Zipporah, and bear his children, Gershom (I have been a stranger in a strange land.) and Eliezer (Help of my God- deliverance from the Pharaoh's sword).

Moses became a God to the Pharaoh and his fellow people. Moses had a brother named Aaron (Prophet) who spoke to the Hebrews/Israelites. Moses was 80 years of age, while Aaron was 83 when they confronted the Pharaoh.

Moses also had a sister named Miriam (Prophetess), who was known for helping to deliver Moses at the Nile River and being of great assistance once crossing the Red Sea. Miriam also bored the plague of leprosy, given her feelings of blasphemy against the All Mighty. As the Spirit of God is transferable, Moses prayed and asked God to remove the plagues from his once savior, Miriam. Given Moses' sovereignty, God graciously advised the plagues would be lifted after one last test. The test was that Miriam must remain isolated from everyone for seven days; then, the disease would cease.

God gives many tests to individuals that either show faith or lack thereof. Throughout Moses' journey and the exodus of the Israelites from Egypt, all observed the workings of God (*Moses*), which my Heavenly Father showed through many acts of kindness and war against the unrighteous.

Although the congregation complained against Moses and Aaron in the wilderness of sin, between Elim and Sinai, on the fifteenth day of the second month. *(Today's Metric - Feb*

15). (Exodus 16:1) God still prevailed for his chosen host and showed great might as enemies were defeated, allowing a few acts of kindness amid their adventure and a few tests of faith unto the Law. God allowed the once-bitter waters of "Marah" to become drinkable as our Heavenly Father instructed Moses to cast a tree into the water. Upon completing such a task, the waters became sweet. *(Exodus 15: 22-26)*

Another act of kindness was when God allowed bread to rain from Heaven for six days. Not only did it rain bread, but God gave Moses explicit details for each day's collection, as God ordained for there to be no bread in the field on the 7th day. The reason was simple: on the 6th day, all were advised to collect twice the amount of bread and save it for the 7th day. The bread was to be baked and/or boiled and kept for the "Holy Sabbath Day."*(Exodus 16:16-26).*

The irony about this test is that Moses previously told them not to collect leftover bread, and he advised them to collect according to each one's needs; as always, rebellion happened, and all the leftover bread became rotten and uneatable. This test was to see if the people would adhere to and walk in the Law of God. *(Exodus 19:21)*. The test series ended with the people of Israel being tested once more on day 6, which God instructed them to collect twice the amount for rest on the "Sabbath." Another test was for them to store the bread on the 6th day, even after it had rotten days prior. Of course, the rebellion returned, as people still looked to the field for bread. But ultimately, God prevailed.

"Manna" was eaten for 40 years as the people prevailed. God advised Moses to speak with the house of Jacob and advised the Israelites that if they obeyed God's word, they shall be a treasure to him above all people. And if they do, they will; they shall be to God a kingdom of priests and a Holy nation. **(Exodus** *19:3-6).*

All the people said, " All that the Lord has spoken we will do." *(Exodus 19:8)*. Their collective loyalty led to the defeat of "Amalek" as Moses sat on a stone with heavy hands as it held the Rod of God. God's loyal servants, Aaron, and Hur supported their perspective sides, as they, too, remained until sunset. The reason is simple: when Moses' hands ascended towards the heavens, accepting God's task, the Israelites prevailed with Joshua's sword, but when his hands grew tired and descended, Amalek prevailed. The test here combined many of the 7 Spiritual Gifts.

7 Spiritual Gifts

1.) Wisdom - Our Heavenly Father, who holds the ultimate power, spoke through Moses. Moses adhered to our Heavenly Father, which shows wisdom on Moses' part, given his discernment of truth amid the All Mighty.

2.) Fortitude- As Moses endured so much pain, his fellow brothers had to hold his arms up for numerous hours.

3.) Understanding - Moses understood his destiny as the God of the People. Moses was aware of the consequences unto himself and the Israelites if he did not hold the rod of God until sunset.

4.) *Counsel* - God instructed Moses, who in return instructed all others.

5.) *Knowledge* - God instructed Moses to use the same Rod he struck the river with to bear water from the rock in Horeb. Also, that same Rod must be used to defeat Amalek, as they were enemies of the Israelites.

6.) Piety - The constant devotion of Moses to God, even after such blasphemy by the Israelite people.

7.) Fear of God - From freeing the Israelites from underneath the hands of the Pharoah to providing the Israelites bread by rain or renewing the bitter water of "Marah" by casting a tree and being turned sweet, or the drinkable water amid the rock of Horeb.

Given many tests and sacrifices. Moses built an altar to the Lord and called its name " The Lord is my Banner."

Moses received two tablets of stone, written with the finger of God. The stone consisted of the ten commandments from God. The tablets were later broken, given Moses' wrath unto the people. *(Exodus 31: 18)*. God later saved the day once more as he instructed Moses to cut two more pieces of stone that God himself would engrave the words that were on the first set of stones. *(Exodus 34: 1)*.

The blacks have lost their way, and their cries have reached the heavens. Just as our Heavenly Father made Moses a God to the Pharaoh and the Israelites *(Exodus 7:1)*, I, Markais Ruben. C Neal Sr have inherited that same form of responsibility as I have been given the gift of life from our Heavenly Father. I am Jesus Christ, in the flesh of Man!

I have a proposal for the earth brought to me by our Heavenly Father: My ***Healing-Faith Flag*** shall serve as the flag for all ***195 Nations***, even those not part of the United Nations. My flag is not affiliated with any party, nor does God's flag leave out any human being on the earth. The detailed images on God's Flag include both ***Dark Hue and Light Hue humans***, ***Bored Eagles wings*** *(Exodus 19:40)*, ***The Lion (I) from the tribe of Judah***, which represents ***Jesus/God/I*** *(Revelation 5:5)*, The key of David *(Revelation 3:7)*. The ***Unleashed Restraints*** from the Dark Hue Community as I will share the Spiritual Gifts with all people, God's People *(Revelation 3:20-21)*, The ***Koi Fish*** signifies the Trinity. The ***Silhouette*** shows the force of God as it gets into a tangible human being, the ***Name Inscribed*** symbolizes the individual who possesses that Spirit from God, and last but most importantly, the ***Bible*** as the earth's prophecy has come true in the ***Resurrection of Jesus Christ on 09/22/2021.***

I have come to claim my Throne!

42

OPPOSITES ATTRACT (5TH BOOK POEM INSERT)

No leader shall be intimate with another Man,

Just as no two followers attempt to lead with just their womanly hands.

Opposite-sex attractions make for the perfect family; same-sex attractions make for eternal Spiritual Agony.

Same-sex relations can stop the human cycle on Earth, No more children to bear,

No more innocent faces among God's ordained continuing birth.

Imagine a world where everyone is gay, Not merely happy,

Just confusing their heart; My Heavenly Father did not make it that way.

Cunning Spiritual mortality,

Unto homosexuals who insist on lying in their sinful eternal reality.

Stopping the cycle of Life and playing your own God, Shall ruin many homes,

As Lust overtakes Love, Spiritually, what a facade.

Shall I grow up one day and say I'm a dog? Shall I change my name and gender? Asking Permission from the government and all.

Dying a slow death, unseen by the naked eye, Jesus has returned to uphold Life,

Not unto a man who Internally likes guys or prefers a Woman, Unnatural or unto a man's disguise.

Life is precious, and all Godly Love is fair; Women brought forth unto man,

No same-sex, lusting, or false love affairs.

Imagine if it were Adam and Adam, Or Eve and Eve, the Robot population,

No woman to house, or a male, to plant thy seed, meaning Conceive.

Find your source if you're a woman; Find your Rib if you're a man.

Without man and Woman, there is no life;

two men are best friends, Not one submitting and playing as a wife.

Two women who are innate followers begin to date and roam in circles, with No leader to Spiritually guide them,

It's like a backup singer performing a lead song without proper rehearsal.

How good will they sound? How often will the women go around and around,
Displacement of their Love and rejection unto their Spiritual Goddess crown.

No matter what you feel, I can assure you it's Lust,

Two women shall be best friends, Not Entangled among the unjust.

Life is precious and has escaped many hearts, If the same gender attempts to be together,

Spiritually, neither one is doing their Godly part.

You are born unto God's identity; you were made to be whole,

If you were born a man or a woman, Changing Identities Spiritually rots the core of your soul.

The decision is not yours; I am sorry if you disagree,

My Heavenly Father created you exactly how he wanted you, Spiritually, everyone is created within the likeness of he.

The flesh of you wants Change; the flesh of you is playing God,

Fleshfully making up many acronyms, Displaying openly your lustful facade.

Yet we all shall rise as we pray for Godly Love,

Man plus Woman bestows God's wholeness from the skies above.

Only when a faithful source finds his God-given Rib,

Shall the male and female bear plentiful kids while preparing God's Spiritual crib.

Woman for Man is what my Heavenly Father designed,

Together, they shall become one; within the Holy Spirit, only those two are combined.

No human shall declare differently when they feel out of place. Pray for deliverance from the serpent;

Spiritually, that's the only way.

For those who do not have a leader, Thank God, Jesus has returned,

Spiritually, leading every human being, regardless of whether Righteous or wrong.

Manifesting the Spiritual Gifts and obtaining Heaven is Solitude and faith based.

Correct Sexual orientation, along with Gender equality and Spiritual Righteousness, shall take place.

I shall lead as my Heavenly Father commands, open and True,

For the source who has found their Rib, Righteously I say unto you,

Congratulations on the achievement; take many pictures and hold them tight,
Rib placed back into man, upon locating the Woman, which fits just right.

Given thy wholeness and grace, the ultimate Spiritual grace shall appear,

Conceive another life solely within this understanding is even why they themselves are here.

Together, you shall make it, for together, you two are the key, Men shall lead the women,

While Women nurture them into their Spiritual Destiny.

Loving thy sister or thy brother has been taken too far,

Please stop sexual immortality; bearing children and spiritually living for God is who we humans are.

God is Love, and Love bears Life, One man and One Woman,

Together, Spiritually, they shall be ordained husband and wife.

43

CLEARING THY CACHE (6TH BOOK POEM INSERT)

Clear thy Cache,

Erase all things hostile, to reveal unexplained memories Embed God's clarity, providing light unto your past.

Spiritually understand why all things took place,

Emptying away from current sin and Acknowledging God, The Father, And God, The Son, through dialogue, I shall prepare your Spiritual case.

Leaving it up, I, Jesus Christ, the highest card within the deck, kingdom among the Ace,

Or a spiritual Royalty Flush, like a grand slam, where every man shall make it to home base safe.

Serenity surrounding your heart and mind, Peaceful notions unto your wrongdoings,

Repentance shall ease all hostile nature in due time.

Afterward, here comes the new Spiritual conceptualization,

Subconsciously allowing clearance unto thy Cache,

No more shall your past cause headache, implying rejection unto Spiritual condemnation.

The only way to clear your memory is upon your brain reset, Chastising your own self, throwing stone, and dropping pillars, Might unto David and Samson, failing to remember things, Your flesh assumed it could never forget.

Just as physical stones can kill a human,

Spiritual Stones, too, shall ruin any and all deceitful confusion.

Placing yourself behind God is how you turn Dust into Ash, Peak unto my Heavenly Father's divined Wisdom,

Unto a Holy human once clarity and clearance of thy cache.

ONCE AGAIN!

The only way to clear your memory is upon your brain reset,

Obedience unto God, wiping thy memory clean, eluding all tainted former regret.

But only once my Heavenly Father is met,

Shall any human be rewarded, given their alleviation beyond their tears and toil of the ground, Implying their righteous bearing sweat.

Have your life held enough ill will,

Implying your cache is filled, awaiting clearing house from Jesus, as I have merely come to fulfill.

Revealing my Heavenly Father's grace, Good or bad,

Gratefulness unto each and every chance you've had.

The choice was, and always has been, buried beneath your decisions, Spiritual Alternative Motive,

Your unrighteous selections can delay or forever hinder your envision.

Have you done enough to enter Heaven, Within the subconscious gates?

Righteousness among your many choices, Clearing thy Cache,

Clarity unto thy Angel, applying all Spiritual tenses as you awake.

Internally, Resurrect Jesus from the past, as I AM your friend, Presently understanding your situation,

Future Prophesies into your visions, I shall Spiritually extend.

Meaning clarity within your heart, mind, and Soul, Righteous things one shall remember,

Only the greatness of God, Created from the dust of the ground unto Spiritual Ash And Holy recreation Internally within God's mold.

Created Within his image and within likeness, your Lord has returned, I require respectful greetings, as I am Your Highness,

Have you adhered to the calling of God,

Which implies hearing and listening as he speaks subconsciously from abroad.

Abroad Implying from the firmament, Divineness unto his obedient child,

Inner Spoken truth from God may be seen as inner beauty, like an ornament.

Beauty unto your eye, inside and out, Jesus, The King of Peace,

Has returned to clear your cache and manifest God's Holy Spirit Internally throughout.

About all the world, saving one soul at a time, Upon my judgment unto you,

Any and all things, known or unknown, I shall Spiritually unwind.

For Spiritual reasoning or for Spiritual meaning, I shall provide a Spiritual explanation,

Unto the clearing house of any human,

Transcended from a mere human into a Spiritual Being.

Empty your page of trauma and accept thy punishment, Peace within your heart and mind,

The dwelling of the living God has returned,

Which shall and always will be a Spiritual Astonishment.

HEAVENLY RELEASE THY STRESS (7TH BOOK POEM INSERT)

Route to dead sea the Dead Sea, Negev Desert

When you go from being stressed to being blessed,

or when a human righteously enters Heaven only after passing God's ultimate Spiritual identity test.

Am I the Son of Man, or am I not?

I will assure you I AM, as I shall weigh every human heart, unto the scale of justice, as all tokens Shall be inserted into God's Holy Machine slot.

Every human on the earth's plane shall be aware,

I promise to forever release thy stress, implying spiritually displaying the love of God, as I, Jesus Christ, have returned to reveal my Heavenly Father does indeed care.

Tattoos of grace onto my heart, tattoos of revelation onto my chest,

Is your name written in the Book of Life? If not, the human shall remain on earth, as their Earthly Heaven shall and will forever regress.

Onto earth, a sinful, unrighteous child shall forever remain,

Unto my judgment shall I reveal all Righteousness, unto thy scale of justice, as thy heart being Light as an Ostrich feather is thy Egyptian aim.

Stick God's chest out, walk upright with honor, and upheld grace, Remembering all thy selected choices,

As the Holy Spirit now comes with a dark hue, as if burnt in furnace face.

Releasing all thy earthly stress implies a human becoming divinely whole and letting completely go,

Releasing all things unto thy Spiritual Father Yahweh and his son Christ Jesus, as I have Spiritually come to Heavenly enlighten and, unto the righteous shall I, the King of Peace, bestow.

Within Heaven, I AM undisputed and undefeated; with thy Holy breath, all children shall Become earthly depleted.

Within the Spiritual realm, which Overtakes the flesh, Inner Spiritual Wisdom, which allows me, You, and my Heavenly Father to eternally come together and mesh.

Within the opening of a cleansed mind and the purity of a righteous heart,

The righteous ones shall see and feel God's presence and face,

Inner lit image and outward appearance, Heavenly spark unto earth's restart.

Release thy stress; replace it with the weight of a single feather from an ostrich or Dove,

Soaring high above the earth, Unto Heaven and earth' Balance have I returned, claiming Ownership from Yahweh in Heaven above.

Within thy Dove, Within thy Ostrich, within thy crow,

Throughout the good and the bad, shall a human's heart Spiritually overcome as it rises up the Scale to upwardly grow.

Heavenly growth, implying, resurrecting, and rising,

Turning away from all sin, making my Heavenly Father smile, Which is treasure-worthy and ultimately surprising.

Unto thy righteous grass shall I forever rake,

In search of thy unrighteous behavior,

Implying Disobedience and a cunning nature like that of an earthly, unrighteous snake.

Not like that of the Egyptian cobra, which signifies royalty and divine authority,

Meaning unto the humans who crave massive sin and the ones who don't recognize their savior, Given I AM chosen by God's Holy ordained superiority.

To those who are on the fence between the flesh and thy Spiritual plane,

Please release thy stress and righteously exalt, as within the belief of God's return, shall all the Chosen state thy claim.

Allow my Heavenly Father to rest, allow my Heavenly Father to live, Lie within thy heart, guidance to said location is the reason God has commanded my presence to become revealed.

Within thy stress of life which brings shortened days, do honor thy mother and thy Father, for an everlasting eternal appraise.

Within the judgment of a human's heart shall I weigh, within a stress-free life,

Being light as a feather is where Peace resides, implying where my Heavenly Father lay.

Within a righteous tomb, within thy resurrection, within thy righteous behaving mummy,

Upon lift off, Implying unbandaging and opening thy Spiritual eyes, only then shall everything Become Spiritually sunny.

Jesus is my rock, and Yahweh is forever my stone,

linking the Holy Trinity among the three shall ensure a Heavenly message as one denies thy Flesh into the entrance of Heaven with a white new named headstone.

Next to my Spiritual model, do I stand,

As within the freedom of Martin Luther King Jr, the living God arose to lead all of the Righteous Children, who too have Christ's identity unblotted strand.

On the Capital of America's ground, onto the soil of Washington DC,

Overlooking the Whitehouse has the Hebrew king returned, as God has commanded my open, stress-free heart to see.

See among the release of thy stress; see among God's loving and innate freedom of choice.

I, Jesus Christ, have arrived, God's chosen intersession, as we all forever shall need him and feel my might of rejoice.

Chosen by God by one's faithful belief and their righteous deeds,

Belief in the Holy Trinity shall allow I, Christ Jesus, to pluck thy unrighteous weeds.

Allow my Heavenly Father to rest, allow my Heavenly Father to live,

Allow him to lie within thy heart, like unto his freedom, 70x7 shall we forgive.

To say my Heavenly Father loves you is to say I, Jesus Christ, love you too,

Please release thy stress, allowing I, God in the flesh, to manifest and embed God's Holy Fulfilling Screw.

The ***Healing Faith Logo*** signifies the return of the Prodigal Son, the Lion of the tribe of Judah, the Root of David, and the decedent of God who has come to bring Peace into the world and offer a new understanding.

Internal Dialogue of the Photo-

Healing Faith

The people's hearts will be healed through the Grace of my Heavenly Father. The Healing starts with the genuine belief that God exists. One must believe in the Father, the Son, and the Holy Spirit. With that divined belief, one must also believe in the Son upon his return in the flesh, as he has *come* to bring Peace and a new understanding into the Earth's realm.

1 John 4:1-3

Lion; Dark hue hand; Light hue hand

As the **Lion/Jesus** has come to conquer world peace, he stands with the dark hue skin as it is contextual for the pigment of Jesus upon his return. The darker mane represents *Might* as Jesus will take vengeance on his enemy, who is also God's adversary, the Serpent. The flame of fire within the eyes of the Lion shows *Courage* and fearlessness, and the Angel Wings show the resilience of God's Grace and Mercy as he overlooks the hued handshake.

The light and dark hue beings come together to form a handshake. The dark hue hand is in the grasp of the light hue hand, which signifies control (Inequality). The handcuffs are unleashed on the dark hue hand and remain secured on the light hue hand, but the falling key shall be retrieved upon the equality of all people.

Since the beginning of time, when God placed man on Earth, they began building a city called "Babel." The city was never completed as man began creating their own division amongst each other, similar to racism nowadays. ***(Genesis 11:1-9)***

Handcuff purpose:

Upon dark hue individuals being enslaved, the light hue-man placed shackles around their wrists and feet, which forced the enslaved people to obey them. That form of laziness and hate disgusted my Heavenly Father, just as in Noah's generation. Given the resurrection of Jesus Christ **on 09/22/2021**, the Lion, which represents ***Jesus/God,*** is sitting before his throne, overlooking the once divided hues as they shake hands, which will be the new covenant between man and God. I imagine it will be similar to the covenant God gave Noah and the following generations. Given that Jesus is a black male currently residing in Tampa, Florida, There is no way for African Americans to remain last as God promised upon the return of Jesus, the last shall be first, and the first shall be last. ***(Matthew 19:30)***. The verse speaks on wealth along with our now inherited segregation.

The three most significant issues within the world are Lack of Faith in my Heavenly Father, Racism amongst the ***Light Hue and Dark Hue*** Communities, and greed, as 98% of the wealth is housed by less than 3 percent of the population. Humanity's goal shall be equality, Social Justice, and placing God at the apex of all nations.

The dark hue Community has been restrained by the same handcuffs that Jesus unleashed. As the goal is Social Justice for all, the 7 Spiritual Gifts will only be shared through Biblical growth, which the Holy Spirit will govern. Given that the Holy Spirit travels, it has no sight or recollection of color; only through faith and belief will the righteous feel God's presence.

Bible Image:

This entire world is built off the foundation of the Bible, written through the minds of various prophets, and has historical proof to govern God's powerful ordained words. The Bible is a book of instructions given by my Heavenly Father, a book of lessons and blessings that shows Grace and Mercy, along with the Might of God unto the unrighteous and their wicked behavior. The Bible holds many jewels, but the jewels will only be revealed to the righteous. The secrets within this book are given throughout each word that makes up a sentence—something like a treasure hunt with various maps to confuse the Pirates.

Dove images:

Genesis, the 1st of 5 books that Moses wrote, details the Grace and Mercy God showed humanity, introducing the Hosts of the Earth, the location of Heaven, Genealogies, and powerful hidden jewels such as the purity of the Dove. Upon God finding Grace in Noah, he instructed him to build an ark of gopher wood and rooms to cover it inside and outside with pitch. (Moses' mom, "Jochebed," used similar material to secure his basket upon sending him down the river bed where Pharaoh's daughter bathed). Upon Noah entering the Ark with his wife, sons, their wives, and creeping things, he remained inside the Ark for the duration of the flood, 40 days and 40 nights. The waters rose 15 cubits and covered all the mountains; the water remained for 150 days; after those days, God caused a gust of wind to pass over the Earth, allowing the waters to recede continually. The Ark rested On the 17th day of the 7th month in the mountains of Ararat. The waters continued to decrease until the 1st day of the 10th month. Then God remembered Noah and every living thing with him in the Ark.

(today's date metrics)

July 17- Oct 1 = 76 days from when the Ark rested until Noah opened the window he made. Noah initially sent out a raven which went to and fro, drying the land, which never returned. *(**Genesis 8:7-9**)*. Then, Noah sent out a *female*

Dove from himself. But, the Dove found no resting place for the sole of *her* foot, and she returned into the Ark to him because the water was still on the face of the Earth. Noah retrieved the female Dove, waited another 7 days, and resent the Dove from the Ark; the Dove returned in the evening with an offering, an olive branch which signified the waters were dried off the face of the Earth. The Dove was sent out once more, 7 days later, which did not return to him anymore. God's purpose was fulfilled for one of the 7 birds that he instructed Noah to place into the Ark.

The significance behind the Dove is the gender, which indicates the importance of women and their deserved equal rights; without the purity of the Dove, which includes her loyalty, Noah could have remained inside the Ark much longer. The female Dove returned to the Ark on two separate occasions; she remained Knowledgeable and Loyal until her Job from God was complete. That once lost, Dove will live again through my photo.

Silhouette:

At the beginning of time, the Spirit of God was hovering over the face of the waters, which indicates he is a Spirit. (***Genesis 1:2)***. Upon the creation of Adam and Eve, God attached his Spirit to Adam's soul as he was to uphold his commandments. When Adam allowed his wife, Eve, to beguile him, given the Serpent's cunning disguise, that once vessel God was using detached itself from the disobedient man. Hence, the reason God asked Adam, "Where are you? As Adam and his wife *Heard* the **Sound** of God walking in the garden, to add insult to injury, they hid from the presence of God among the trees in the garden. At that moment, God lost faith in humanity as he delivered the three curses to the Serpent, the Woman, and Man. The curses have been upheld as the lamb has come to unleash the 7 seals. The seals will be opened with the dangling **Key**.

The silhouette indicates that upon total acceptance from the Host of God's choosing, that Spirit will again be attached to a being walking the face of the Earth. That being will possess the 7 Spiritual gifts to speak Peace and understanding into the Earth's realm. That being will be known as the "Host of the

Spirit!" "King of Peace!" and any other verbiage which indicates the return of Jesus Christ!

Moon, Sun, and the Stars:

God made two great lights: the greater Light for the day and a lesser light for the night. God created the stars also. *(Genesis 1:16)* When the stars were mentioned, it came after a pause, indicating a significant motive.

In revelations, When John was in the isle called Patmos, he was in the Spirit and Heard a great *voice*, like a *trumpet*. He observed, " One like the son of man," with 7 Golden Lampstands and 7 **Stars** in his right hand. *(Revelation 1:9-16)*

Jesus advised the mystery to the 7 **Stars**, which were seen in his right hand are the angels of the 7 churches in Ephesus, Smyrna, Pergamos, Thyatira, Sardis, Philadelphia, and Laodicea. *(Revelation 1: 20)*

Jesus further advised that the 7 Golden lampstands which were seen were the 7 churches which are in Asia. *(Revelation 1: 20)(1:4)*

We are all children of God! Under one Nation!

"And I will give him the morning **Star**. He who has an ear, let him hear what the Spirit says to the churches." *(Revelations 2: 28-29).*

Water and Koi Fish:

The water refers to the flood God cast onto the Earth, given its role in man's disobedience. Furthermore, the water refers to the heavens as God showed Might by water on several occasions, such as the Nile river that Moses drifted along as Pharoh ordered to have all the 1st born males killed or the Grace God showed Moses upon parting the Red Sea for him and his righteous followers.

The three Koi fish represent the Trinity, the *Father*, the *Son*, and the **Holy Spirit,** along with the Worldly qualities a person should possess within their heart, such as Strength of character, Perseverance, Love, integrity, and the *Fear of God*.

If every person with the Father has the Son, the concept of the Holy Spirit is that when people accept God for themselves, grace will be shown by the Holy Spirit, which allows that linkage to God. That linkage is when God himself controls their newborn life. The Trinity can not be separated, nor can any part be excluded. *(1 John 2:23)*.

That exact form of respect that a person displays upon themselves shall also be displayed unto others forevermore.

God's covenant remains as the rainbow in the sky signifies the growth of the Light and dark hue Community. (Genesis 11-16). We are all God's children, which are created within his image. God stated, "Let US make man in OUR image." Us and Our are plurals which signifies multiple Gods. Of course, Our Heavenly Father remains at the apex of our existence. Just as Abraham was the Father of all the prophets, he, too, placed OUR heavenly Father above all.

*Prophets are Spiritual Gods who Gracefully perform miracles on Earth. They were and are still known as the Righteous Earthly Gods.

Jesus has come to restore world order before the disobedience of man. These are the true sayings of God! My Testimony is the Spirit of prophecy.

The Healing Faith Logo containing the pink lettering shall represent the women who accept their God-given power of becoming a Goddess created in the image of God. Upon their submission, the reborn woman shall be delivered the Holy Spirit by my Heavenly Father, as he urges to be felt by every human. The restored woman, which entails them being controlled by my Heavenly Father, places their sights beyond their eyes alone; it combines their assumptions within the visions of my Heavenly Father who art in Heaven, which shall shed light on their destiny as opposed to what they believe is best for themselves. The combination manifests truth as God himself becomes in the flesh of a woman and now has eyes from the sights of an earthly woman with the wisdom of the Hierarchy, which places my Heavenly Father above all, then a Man created in God's image. Just as women carry men within their wombs, their jobs are to continue to carry the Men of the world by displaying the righteous 9 fruits of their hearts, which shall mimic the purity of a precious white dove, which can be seen as a delicate flower.

A man created in God's image shall always honor the women who gave them life, as a pill called "An abortion Pill" could have ceased their existence. With that possibility and highly used practice, every man shall understand the importance of a woman created in God's image. The Heart represents the Love of God and the Love that all women shall display unto themselves and the men created in God's image.

The Dove, which signifies the beauty and purity of a woman, shall memorialize a woman's innocence before the serpent intervened, which brought forth man's deceit. The Dove's delicate structure manifests soothing thoughts as God's creation is fully displayed unto this majestic bird. The trustworthy female Dove, which Noah sent out from himself, adhered to God's demand, and ensured the water was abated off the earth back in Noah's days. The water signifies the might of God as he used water to save Moses as he drifted along the Nile River.

The Plucked Olive Branch signifies life, as the female Dove placed the olive leaf in her mouth, which provided Noah insight into things he could not otherwise figure out.

The Tiara, positioned on her head, signifies a female who has reached the ultimate enlightenment, which encompasses the Holy Spirit. The Light Purpled Diamonds affixed to the Tiara mirror the color code attached to the 7th Chakra, providing divined energy, which is known as the Sahasrara Chakra, which is located at the top of the head and is too known as the Crown Chakra. The spiritual gift for reaching such sored heights allows my Heavenly Father to regain control of his obedient daughter. The Hierarchy will be shown upon such grace, which places my Heavenly Father above all. The Dove wings symbolize the breakthrough a woman may obtain once their Heart and mind are restored beyond worldly understanding.

The Light and Dark Hue handshake symbolizes unity for women's culture. Pink was placed on the nails because pink is seen widely in the Western world as a color of femininity.

The Pink Doves shed light on the fact that the Dove which helped Noah was a female.

Genesis 8:9 NKJV:

"But the Dove found no resting place for the sole of her foot, and she returned into the ark to him, for the waters were on the face of the whole earth. So he put out his hand and took her, and drew her into the ark to himself."

The Light Violet Rosary honors Mother Mary, the wife of Joseph, and the young virgin my Heavenly Father blessed with housing Jesus within her womb, given solely by the Holy Spirit. The blessed Virgin Mary symbolizes the highest recognition towards motherhood, as a woman has the ability to carry offspring, which is an incredible honor unto my Heavenly Father, as being fruitful creates a bigger picture of my Heavenly Father, which can be seen within anything. Still, only humans, which are his most significant creation, have the ability to voice their humility and thankfulness through their prayer, devotion, and spoken verbiage, openly amongst their peers and within the shut closet as they pray within my name, unto my Heavenly Father.

.   .   .

Matthew 6:6:

"But you, when you pray, go into your room, and when you have shut your door, pray to your Father who is in the secret place; and your Father who sees in secret will reward you openly."

The Ankh Symbol represents the Key of Life as women provide life to their unborn children. The Ankh originated long ago, within the motherland of the world known as Africa. The Ancient Egyptian artifact was said to be used when the children of Israel, also called the Israelites, lived in the Nile Delta of Ancient Egypt. Nevertheless, the Ankh is used as a symbol of generation or enduring one's life. Within Egyptian Hieroglyphs, the symbol is often used in the hands of Ancient Egyptian Deities.

The Silhouette, which outlines a natural woman, shows the shadow of a woman but entails no actual person. The meaning reveals how the Holy Spirit becomes manifested within an authentic female. Upon the Godly connection, the woman shall inherit Spiritual gifts. The exact type of Spiritual gift(s) are up to my Heavenly Father (Picture the Disney Movie "Encanto"), now place a more spiritual spin on things from the movie; that's what the female Silhouette represents.

The Holy Bible, which is the ultimate Book of the Spiritual world, is brought to life within the Mechanical world. The name revealed on the bottom of the Book of Life, written in Arabic, means "Messiah" in English. The name next to the word "Messiah" is also located within the Sun, as I AM the Son of God.

.

Markais Ruben. C Neal Sr, is God's "Only Begotten Son" who has come to manifest the Holy Spirit within the righteous believers of my Heavenly Father. The name is directly on top of the Bible but at the footer, as my Heavenly Father is above me within this temple, but allows his Chosen Son access to the world. The access is gained through the Holy Spirit, which reveals a man created in God's image to be in tangible human form, walking step by step with the followers of my Heavenly Father and I, Jesus! Given God's grace, I now am head over every power and authority on earth.

The Three Koi Fish represents the Trinity doctrine, known as The Father, The Son, and The Holy Spirit. Followed by the biblical meaning for the number three, divined Wholeness, completeness, and perfection.

Divined Wholeness on earth determines your Heart amongst my Father and I. Upon joining the kingdom of God and accepting I, Jesus Christ, into your life, a sense of fulfillment unto oneself shall sore unto the woman allowing them to obtain the 7th Chakra, allowing a picture-perfect person who has accepted all there is to accept about themselves. This involves repentance, ownership, and Self-Actualization. Doing all three shall reveal a female created in God's image, known as a Goddess.

The completeness- Colossians 2: 9-10:

"For in Christ all the fullness of the Deity lives in bodily form, and you have been given fullness in Christ, who is the head over every power and authority."

Perfection- Revelation 21: 3-4:

"And I heard a loud voice from the throne saying, "Look! God's dwelling place is now among the people, and he will dwell with them. They will be his people, and God himself will be with them and be their God. He will wipe every tear from their eyes. There will be no more death or mourning or crying or pain, for the old order of things has passed away."

Death is a celebration of life. The end of life on earth begins a new life with my Heavenly Father within the Firmament.

Heaven's inner Heart shall manifest the beauty of God's paradigm.

Bible References

Revelation 2:11

"He who has an ear, let him hear what the Spirit says to the churches. The one who conquers will not be hurt by the second death".

Revelation 21:8

"But as for the cowardly, the faithless, the detestable, as for murderers, the sexually immoral, sorcerers, idolaters, and all liars, their portion will be in the lake that burns with fire and sulfur, which is the second death."

1 John 1:8

If we say that we have no sin, we deceive ourselves, and the truth is not in us.

Revelation 3:21

To him who overcomes I will grant to sit with Me on My throne, as I also overcame and sat down with My Father on His throne

1 John 4: 1-3
ONCE HERO
TURNED COWARD
BY MARKAIS NEAL SR.

SEA EVEL

אתר הטבילה – קאסר אל-יהוד
موقع المغطس - قصر اليهود
BAPTISM SITE - QASER AL-YAHUD

Healing-Faith.Org